AN IN-DEPTH STUDY ON MOTOR CREATIVITY IN TEENAGE STUDENTS

JULY, 2012

ACKNOWLEDGEMENT

The investigator is indebted directly or indirectly to all those from whom and from whose works help have been taken. Some of course deserve special mention.

The investigator expresses her deepest gratitude to her supervisor Dr. Sanjib Mridah, Associate Professor of the Department of Physical Education, University of Kalyani, whose critical and constructive suggestions and inspiring guidance enabled to accomplish the hard task of investigation with such an off-beat study and to present this thesis in a worthwhile shape.

The investigator renders her grateful thanks to all the teachers of the Physical Education Department whose valuable suggestions helped her to overcome some of the difficulties faced by her during the investigator.

The investigator expresses her grateful thanks to retired Prof. Durgadas Bhattacharya of the Department of Education, University of Kalyani for his valuable suggestions during the course of her investigation.

To Pallab Kumar Mondal, Physical Education Teacher of Satminsha High School, Diamond Harbour for the investigator owes deep indebtedness for his help in the statistical treatment required for this study.

The investigator expresses her sincere thanks to Dr. Debasish Roy, Lecturer of Mugberia College of Physical

Education, to Parima Ghosh and to the members of District School Sports Association, Murshidabad for their technical assistance and kind co-operation during the collection of data.

The investigator expresses sincere thanks to the Headmaster, Headmistress and other teachers of the schools concerned, where the investigations were done, for their kind permission and co-operation in conducting the research work.

Without the encouragement from my loving daughter Drishti and my beloved husband Bijoy Kumar Ghosh, I could not have even attempted to undertake such a project. So the researcher is really thankful to them.

And lastly the investigator acknowledges with deep satisfaction the hearty co-operation extended by the subjects of this study in conducting the investigations.

Date : 17·07·12

(Santwana Goon)

CONTENTS

	Page No.
CHAPTER – I : INTRODUCTION	1 – 14
1.1 General Introduction	1
1.2 Demographic Correlates of Creativity	2
1.2.1 Age and Creativity	2
1.2.2 Gender and Creativity	3
1.2.3 Locale, Culture and Creativity	4
1.3 Creativity and Influencing Factors	5
1.4 Creativity and Motor Creativity	8
1.5 Statement of the Problem	10
1.6 Purpose of the Study	10
1.7 Significance of the Study	11
1.8 Delimitation of the Study	11
1.9 Limitation	12
1.10 Definition of Terms and Explanation of the Concepts	12
1.10.1 Motor Creativity	12
1.10.2 Intelligence	13
1.10.3 Achievement Motivation	13
1.10.4 Academic Achievement	14
CHAPTER – II : REVIEW OF RELATED LITERATURE	15 – 30
CHAPTER – III : METHODOLOGY	31 – 47
3.1 Introduction	31
3.2 Subjects	31
3.3 Criteria Measured	33
3.3.1 Tools and techniques used for data collection	34
3.4 Administration of the Tests for Data Collection	35

	Page No.
3.5 Motor Creativity Tests	36
3.5.1(a) Motor Creativity Test Item No. I	37
3.5.1 (b) Motor Creativity Test Item No. II	37
3.5.1(c) Motor Creativity Test Item No. III	37
3.5.1(d) Motor Creativity Test Item No. IV	38
3.5.1(e) Motor Creativity Test Item No. V	38
3.6 Test of Intelligence	43
3.6.1 Scoring and Administration of Intelligence Test	44
3.7 Test of Achievement Motivation	45
3.7.1 Scoring and administration of Achievement Motivation Test	46
3.8 Academic Achievement	56
3.8.1 Procedure of Data Collection	46
3.9 Design of the Study	46
3.10 Statistical Method used for the Study	46
CHAPTER – IV : RESULTS AND DISCUSSION	**48 – 92**
4.0 Organization	48
CHAPTER – V : SUMMARY, CONCLUSION AND RECOMMENDATION	**93 – 101**
5.1 Summary	93
5.2 Conclusion	99
5.3 Recommendations	101
BIBLIOGRAPHY	**102 – 109**
APPENDICES	**110 – 142**

LIST OF TABLES

Table No.	Particulars	Page No.
1	Distribution of Subjects	32
2	The subjects selected from the Schools	33
3	Format showing the Details of the Intelligence Test	44
4	Format showing the Factors of Achievement Motivation	45
5	Descriptive Statistics of Motor Creativity and its Components for 13 Years Age Group	49
6	Descriptive Statistics of Motor Creativity and its Components for 14 Years Age Group	50
7	Descriptive Statistics of Motor Creativity and its Components for 15 Years Age Group	51
8	Descriptive Statistics of Motor Creativity and its Components for 16 Years Age Group	52
9	Descriptive Statistics of Motor Creativity and its Components for 17 Years Age Group	54
10	Descriptive Statistics of Motor Creativity and its Components for 18 Years Age Group	55
11	Descriptive Statistics of Motor Creativity and its Components on Boys and Girls Group	56

Table No.	Particulars	Page No.
12	Three-way ANOVA on MC_1 (Flexibility)	60
13	Pairwise comparison among Group Means of MC_1 (Originality)	61
14	Three-way ANOVA on MC_2 (Flexibility)	61
15	Pairwise comparison among Group Means of MC_2 (Flexibility)	63
16	Three-way ANOVA on MC_3 (ISP)	63
17	Pairwise comparison among Group Means of MC_3 (ISP)	64
18	Three-way ANOVA on MC_4 (Fluency)	65
19	Pairwise comparison among Group Means of MC_4 (Fluency)	66
20	Three-way ANOVA on MC_5 (Elaboration)	67
21	Pairwise comparison among Group Means of MC_5 (Elaboration)	68
22	Three way ANOVA of MCT	68
23	Pairwise Comparison among Group Means of MCT	69
24	Pairwise comparison of Motor Creativity according to Gender	70
25	Descriptive Statistics of Motor Creativity for Early and Late Adolescent Groups	71
26	Three-way ANOVA on MC_1 (Originality) of Early and Late Adolescent Groups	73

Table No.	Particulars	Page No.
27	Pairwise comparison among the group means of MC_1 for early and late adolescent boys and girls	74
28	Three-way ANOVA of MC_2 (Flexibility) of Early and Late Adolescent Group	75
29	Pairwise comparison among the group means of MC_2 for early and late adolescent boys and girls	76
30	Three-way ANOVA of MC_3 (ISP) of Early and Late Adolescent Group	77
31	Pairwise comparison among the group means of MC_3 of Early and Late Adolescent Groups	78
31	Three-way ANOVA of MC_4 (Fluency) of Early and Late Adolescent Groups	78
33	Pairwise comparison among the group means of MC_4 of Early and Late Adolescent Groups	80
34	Three-way ANOVA of MC_5 (Elaboration) of Early and Late Adolescent Groups	80
35	Pairwise comparison among the group means of MC_5 for early and late adolescent boys and girls	81
36	Three way ANOVA of MCT of Early and Late Adolescent Groups	82

Table No.	Particulars	Page No.
37	Pairwise comparison among the group means of MCT for early and late adolescent boys and girls	83
38	ANOVA results of Motor Creativity according to Six Age Groups	84
39	ANOVA results of Motor Creativity of Early and Late Adolescent Groups	85
40	Correlation Matrix on Motor Creativity and other three variables of Early Adolescent Boys and Girls	86
41	Correlation Matrix on Motor Creativity and other three variables of Late Adolescent Boys and Girls	87
42	Correlation Matrix on Motor Creativity and other three variables of Boys and Girls group	88
43.	Correlation Matrix on Motor Creativity and other three variables of the total group	89
44.	Multiple Correlation and Regression Equations for Girls group	91
45.	Multiple Correlation and Regression Equations for Boys group	91

LIST OF FIGURES

Figure No.	Particulars	Page No.
1	Showing the diagram of the course of test item II	37
2	Showing the diagram of the course of test item IV	38
3	Showing the diagram of the course of test item V	39
4	Performing Motor Creativity Test Item No. I	40
5	Performing Motor Creativity Test Item No. II	40
6	Performing Motor Creativity Test Item No. III	41
7	Performing Motor Creativity Test Item No. IV	41
8	Performing Motor Creativity Test Item No. V	42
9	Subjects conferring Written Test on Intelligence	42
10	Subjects conferring Written Test on Achievement Motivation	43
11	Graphical Representation of MC_1 (Originality)	57
12	Graphical Representation of MC_2 (Flexibility)	57
13	Graphical Representation of MC_3 (ISP)	58
14	Graphical Representation of MC_4 (Fluency)	58
15	Graphical Representation of MC_5 (Elaboration)	59
16	Graphical Representation of MCT	59

CHAPTER – I
INTRODUCTION

1.1 General Introduction

Practically everything we do from the time we stretch in the morning until we lie down again for sleep at night is the result of changing muscular movements. These are all motor acts. Movement is so generally observable in living organisms that it has attracted the attention of man as far back as we have a record of his philosophic and scientific interests in himself and the world about him. Movement is as natural and innate a quality as creativity. Man has shown very many ways of creative expressions. These creative movements are as natural, innate and nurture-able as intelligence, imagination and motivation. Creativity, intelligence and motivation are the guiding forces behind man's superior behaviour, expression and contributions.

Creativity has been attributed variously to intuitive intervention, cognitive processes, social environment and personality traits. Creativity connotes the idea of producing something new - a new skill, a solution to a problem or a new philosophy of life.

Creativity is the process of bringing something new into being. Creativity requires passion and commitment. It brings to our awareness what was previously hidden and points to new life. The experience is one of heightened consciousness, towards ecstasy (May, 1974). The ability to transcend traditional ideas, rules, patterns, relationships or the like and to create meaningful new ideas, forms, methods, interpretations etc. is creativity. Creativity is the manifestation of intellect. The amazing ability enables a person to find solutions to challenging problems and makes life worth living. The urge to creativity is universal. It is a special aptitude. Each creation involves a new association of existing elements or a discovered effect. "It is a general constellation of supporting intellectual and personality traits and problem solving traits that help expression of creative behaviour in individual" (Roy, 1984).

Creativity is that act of combining previously unconnected ideas, information and elements to make something new and appropriate (Kellor, 1971).

Human creativity may prove to be the key to success or failure in mankind's quest for knowledge, in his journey beyond the bounds, of the sure and the known, in his exploration of the unknown.

Many movements are creative and imaginative in the field of physical activity and sports. The changes in the techniques of putting the shot or of high jumping, or diving or of gymnastics are but creative expressions of imaginative persons who possess adequate control of their bodily movements along with their creative imaginations.

Imagination is an important element in creativity. Creative imagination is the basis of making inroads into the realms of the unknown. As a child grows, his imaginative thinking grows simultaneously, and has a close relationship (Sharma, 2000).

The flow of creative impulse and the cultivation of creative behaviour is apparently influenced by age and gender.

1.2 Demographic Correlates of Creativity

Biographical variables and socio-cultural climate largely affect the thinking process and shape the personality dispositions of an individual. Investigators have examined the relevance of demographical variables in the development of creativity. Some of the effective demographical variables with which the relationships of creativity are established are age, gender, locale, culture, etc.

1.2.1 Age and Creativity

Age provides biological maturity and traces developmental growth. 'Development of creative thinking' presents a detailed account of 'age' and its relationship with as well as effect on 'creativity'. As such, age is an organic factor that accounts for biological growth and reflects upon the developmental perspective of creativity (Sharma, 2000). While trying to find relationship between age and creativity it has found that creativity increases with age up to certain age level beyond which it starts decreasing (Sansanwal & Jarial, 1980) but the optimum age level has not yet been determined. Creativity scores have been found positively as well as negatively related to age and the developmental trend of creative abilities among males and females have been observed a differential trend of development, indicating thereby the appearance and increase of creativity at different age levels and in different group of people at different period of life in different forms (Jarial, 1983). Development of creativity from infancy to adolescence observes dips at various age levels and those dips are at the age of five, nine and twelve years. These decline of creativity during developmental years of children, have been accounted for new demands of the community for conformity (Torrance, 1962). Each of the dip age levels has its specific significance so far as the adjustment of the child with his new social, cultural or educational demand is concerned. The first dip is at the age of five causes due to initiation of conscious interaction with the external world. The second dip, at the age of nine, causes due to the demand of peer group approval. And the third dip, at the age of twelve, attributes the demands of self identification at the inset of adolescence. Studies on the Australian, German, Indian and American children, who are brought up in the developing, achieving and competitive society, show dips in creativity at various age levels, depicting an irregular creative-growth-curve (Sharma, 2000). Lifespan psychologists have conducted developmental studies of creative people in the arts and the sciences and inferred that at the onset of starting a career to the end, productivity due to creative thoughts, increases rapidly, levels off at a peak, productive age and then slowly declines. Creativity is a two step process i) registers the formation of ideas of a person and ii) transformation and translation of those ideas into action (Simonton, 1983). Creativity, thus, exists as a lifelong cognitive process; however, it does not observe a linear regular developmental growth pattern. It displays a curvilinear relationship with age (Sharma, 2000).

1.2.2 Gender and Creativity

Studies conducted on the individuals of different cultures concluded into three categories of results. Those are – i) superiority of males over females, ii) superiority of females over males, and iii) no significant gender differences in creativity (Jarial, 1983).

Male students of different grades are shown to be excelled than females in almost all tests of verbal and particularly of non-verbal tests of creativity (Torrance, 1965; Torrance & Aliotti, 1969). In semantic flexibility of the students from elementary school to middle school level the males are superior to the females (Guildford, 1964). Males are superior to females in creativity observed by the researchers of our country (Prakash, 1966; Raina, 1971; Rawat & Agarwal, 1977) and from abroad (Kelley, 1965; Middents, 1961). Grade VII and IX male students are superior to their female counterparts in flexibility (Prakash, 1966), in non-verbal elaboration (Middents, 1961), in originality on Torrance Test of Creative Thinking (Raina, 1971; Dhir, 1973) and also in verbal creativity (Jain, 1972; Rawat & Agarwal, 1977). Males are comparatively superior to females in fluency and originality components of creativity (Awasthi, 1979).

In female population, after the age of nineteen years, females consistently excelled males on all aspects of creativity (Torrance, 1967). Females are superior to males in the fluency component of creativity (Piers et al., 1960), in imaginative component (Das, 1959), in originality (Goralski, 1964), in ideational associational and spontaneous forms of fluency (Guilford, 1964). Females are superior than males have observed by the Indian researchers in verbal creativity (Passi, 1971), originality (Raina, 1971), fluency and flexibility (Ripudaman, 1973), verbal and non-verbal creativity (Bedi, 1974). Superiority of females has also been observed in various aspects of creativity, by and large, on Torrance Test of Creative Thinking and Passi Test of Creativity (Sharma, 2000).

Females match males and vice-versa in various aspects of creativity in a wide range of individuals from school going children to elderly aged (Goralski, 1964; Wallach & Kogan, 1965; Kloss, 1972). In Indian context the findings also follow similar patterns (Dutta, 1977; Arora, 1978; Goyal, 1973). Indian researchers do not differ in any aspect of creativity of males and females (Sharma, 2000).

Creativity in respect to gender yields divergent conclusions. Studies conducted on gender difference in creativity reveal not only "no gender difference" between males and females but difference may exist in some aspects of creativity at a certain period of life – the male excelled the females in certain aspects whereas in other aspects at another period the females surpass the males (Sharma, 2000). As many as three probable reasons are account for the discrepancy between two genders' creativity during life time in general and growth period in particular, these are – i) socio-cultural factors within and outside home, ii) differences in attitudes perception and personality traits between them, and iii) differences in the rates of maturation (Taylor, 1969). Socio-cultural restrictions to females at home and in society put greater obstruction in the higher attainment of creative potentiality (Kogan, 1974). The bio-social maturity that the males and females, boys and girls, men and women attain at different cross-sections of the developmental period accounts for their psychological differentiation and 'creative thinking abilities' cannot be an exception to these developmental trends in abilities, aptitudes, traits and talents (Sharma, 2000).

1.2.3 Locale, Culture and Creativity

Locale connotes cultural variation accounted in terms of territorial differences. Locale is one of the most important components that generate cultural variation. Children brought up and nurtured in different locale and cultures, in different social settings adopt differential pattern of personality traits which may have a facilitative or an inhibitory effect on the acquisition and development of creative abilities (Sharma, 2000). Creativity by its very nature requires both sensitivity and independence, and in the culture of the most of the parts of the world, sensitivity is regarded as feminine virtue and independence is a masculine (Torrance, 1962). Only divergent personality maintains both the sensitivity and independence of mind necessary for high level of creative thinking. The role differences between genders are the consequences of variation in social system and cultural values. In rural urban comparison three different results yielded by the researchers – i) no difference in creativity among students of rural and urban area, ii) children belong to urban locale are superior than rural areas (Singh, 1979; Passi, 1971) and iii) rural people are higher than the urban people (Sukla & Sharma, 1978). Studies reveal significant effect of locale as a cultural variation on creativity; however, the superiority of the people of one group can hardly be ascertained due to scarcity of related studies (Passi, 1982). Disadvantaged urban students are more spontaneous in their behaviour and actions, less conformity, more independent of their parents, and more highly developed in motor skills than individuals from advantaged families (Rogers, 1968). Life experiences play important role in the children from low economic status whether brought up in urban or in rural locale for their creative achievement. Children who live in poverty and experience related disadvantages have to struggle for survival and this struggle poses a constant challenge to their creative potential so that they are likely to develop these activities to an even higher degree than their more advantaged and affluent peers (Torrance, 1979).

1.3 Creativity and Influencing Factors
a) Intelligence

Creativity is divergent thinking process whereas intelligence has been associated with 'convergent thinking' (Guilford, 1950); and this conceptual difference provides independent frame of reference for both these cognitive variables as two independent components between which relationship can be established (Foster, 1971). The view has also been supported by many researchers that intelligence tests provide convincing conditions for measuring convergent thinking abilities and not the divergent ones (Torrance, 1962; Getzels & Jackson, 1962). Summarization of all the available evidences as regards the question of the relationship of creativity to intelligence by tabulating 178 coefficients of correlation shows a median correlation of 0.20. When creativity scores are grouped according to the nature of the test is primarily verbal or non-verbal, the median of 88 coefficients between intelligence and verbal creativity is 0.21, and the median of 114 coefficients of correlation between intelligence and non-verbal creativity is 0.06 (Torrance, 1967).

The intellectual achievements can not be achieved without physical efficiency (Sheldon, 1942; Breckenridge & Vincent, 1955; Steinhaus, 1964; Doman, 1968 & Altman, 1968). An individual who "exercises his limbs" should be an intellectual individual; the weak, the unhealthy and the un-playful cannot be as intelligent as the former (Kamalesh, 1982). Intelligence has a direct connection with our mental processes and motor functions which ultimately depend on the efficient functioning of the organic systems of the body. The findings obtained from early studies reveal that the relationships between intelligence and creativity in any of the three kinds, namely – positive, negative or zero relationship. In the long past the indices have been estimated as positive correlation to the extent of 0.15, 0.02 and 0.03 between intelligence and imagination (Andrews, 1930) and a positive low correlation has also predicted between creativity and intelligence (Guilford, 1957). The review result between intelligence and creativity relationship has observed from 178 correlation coefficients with the median correlation to the extent of 0.20 only (Torrance, 1967). These findings support the existence of low positive relationship between creativity and intelligence. There other views hold the notion that creativity and intelligence are positively and significantly correlated to each other, however after reaching a certain limit both of these abilities function independently (Anderson, 1960).

There are numerous studies that indicate creativity as the negative correlates of intelligence (Flascher, 1963; Das, 1959; Rawat & Agarwal, 1977; Safaya, 1981; Khire, 1971; Satyanarayan, 1979). Apart from that there are evidences of zero relationship between two variables, i.e. between creativity and intelligence (Mackinnon, 1962).

The experimental studies on 'Creativity and Intelligence' done under four conditions that is Hi-Hc, Li-Lc, Li-Hc and Hi-Lc reveal that (i) creativity in the children is present in the content of high or low intelligence and (ii) intelligence in the children is present in conjunction with low or high creativity (Wallach & Kogan, 1965).

Researchers believe that creativity involves factors governing "Divergent Thinking" and transformation ability as contrasted to 'Convergent Thinking' for traditional intelligence (Torrance, 1962; Guilford, 1967). People possess high creativity rarely have low IQ, whereas high IQ is often associated with low creativity (Guilford, 1967). It is therefore concluded that "high intelligence" is no longer a guarantee for high creativity; however, a minimum level of intelligence is essentially needed for being a creative individual. Creativity is a different aspect of mental functioning and is independent of the conventional intelligence. Although creativity requires a certain level of intelligence, intelligence alone does not guarantee its presence.

b) Achievement Motivation

Achievement motivation is an important element in creativity. It is seen in general that people who are achievement motivated have a significantly higher chances of progressing their work compared to the other people. Some of the important motivational factors that influence creativity are: (i) the desire to question, (ii) high intellectual persistence and perseverance, (iii) a delight in thinking and toying with ideas (iv) the need for variety (v) insatiable curiosity, (vi) tolerance for ambiguity, (vii) high energy and vast output of work. The three aspects have been accounted for achieve motivation are – (i) a creative attitude, an urge to explore and to explain, a stage of curiosity, (ii) a critical attitude the inclination to search for defects and criticize, a stage of evaluation, (iii) confidence in one's perceptions and willingness to acceptability, a stage of self-confidence and acceptability (Torrance et. al, 1969).

Individuals who exhibit high achievement motivation tend to be promoted more. Teachers having high achievement motivation values show greater scientific productivity than their colleagues who are having low achievement motivation (Mukherjee, 1964). Teachers, who score high on the fluency dimension of creativity, score remarkably higher on the creative motivation scale of the Torrance Personal-Social Motivation Inventory (Raina, 1969). Further it is found that students who score higher on the four dimensions of creativity namely fluency, flexibility originality and elaboration, score significantly higher than the low creative students in the creative motivation scale. The low creative group scored significantly higher than the high creative group on the critical motivational scale. However there is no significant difference between the two groups on Power Motivation Scale (Raina, 1969).

c) Academic Achievement

The interaction effects of creativity and IQ focuses that achievement is predicted better by IQ than by creativity (Bowers, 1969). There is a possibility of discrimination between the high and the low academic achievers on the basis of creativity after pertaining out the effects of IQ (Gopley, 1967). Positive relationship exists between academic achievement and creativity (Taylor, 1965; Gopley & Field, 1969; Gupta, 1969; Khire, 1971; Trivedi, 1969; Raina, 1968). A positive relationship exists between creativity and students' achievement in English and Science subjects, whereas no relationship exists with other subjects (Parmesh, 1973). Positive relationships do exist between fluency and flexibility components of creativity with academic achievement (Dhariwal & Saini, 1976). Relatively, negative relationship between creativity and academic achievement has been reported in very few studies. There exists a negative relationship between science subjects and composite verbal and non-verbal creativity (Bagga, 1973).

Insignificant relationship has revealed in the scholastic attainments despite a difference of 23 points in mean IQ of Hc and Hi groups. (Gatzels & Jackson, 1962). No relationship exists between creativity and academic achievement (Tandraphat, 1976). The similar no relationship condition has also been revealed between creativity and academic achievement (Torrance, 1959; Bist, 1964; Parmesh, 1973; Joshi, 1974). By and large, the occurrence of positive relationship indicates the relationship between creativity and various components of academic achievements: however, the extent and nature of relationship between them depend upon the criteria and kind of scholastic attainment. Relation between creativity and academic achievement is 'curvilinear' in nature; and it yields scatter plot indicating 'high' creativity rarely with low academic achievement while high academic achievement is often associated with low creativity (Dunn, 1962). So, creativity and academic achievement do relate in different ways.

1.4 Creativity and Motor Creativity

In any kind of human endeavour creativity may exercise influence. All can be creative in their respective field of work. A man may thus be creative in motor behaviour, in performing motor movements. Such creativity acts are produced not only by a genius, this quality may be present in the multifarious acts at varying levels of ability. A creative person regroups ideas by means of his own thoughts or actions rather than simply imitating.

The fertile field where creativity may grow is around the situations where there are opportunities to execute skilful movement-oriented activity. Children in their own world of movement and action express their creativeness through play. Motor creativity involves a search for new movements in new situations of the perceptual field, synthesis and inventions. It is a restricting of the perceptual field.

Many movements are creative and imaginative in the field of activity and sports. The changes in the techniques of putting the shot or of high jumping, or diving or of gymnastics are but creative expressions of imaginative persons who posses adequate control of their bodily movements along with their creative imaginations. Creativity consists of eight components namely - originality, flexibility, fluency, elaboration, ingenious solution to problems (ISP), creative production, sensitivity to problems and redefinitions (Tiwari, 1994). Motor Creativity, as it is expressed through creative motor movements, perhaps constitutes more or less those components either any one or a combination of the components of creativity during its execution. Studies are also conducted on different creativity aspects like kinetic flexibility, fluency and originality (Theodora, 2003).

In this study each of the five motor creativity components corresponds to five creativity components, namely – MC_1 to originality, MC_2 to flexibility, MC_3 to ISP, MC_4 to fluency and MC_5 to elaborations. Originality component refers to the unusual ideas and suggestions for unusual applications of particular object with uncommonness or newness. In this study originality in motor creativity has measured through MC_1 where the subjects are to be performed the movements of the upper part of the body as many variations as possible while keeping the lower body part fixed.

Flexibility component measures how many distinct different ways an individual can respond to a stimulus. Flexibility in motor creativity has measured by the number of ways a subject can move (except walking) in a 10-feet distance course, from one line to the other and back which represents MC_2.

ISP measures inventiveness of a person in a given rigid situation. In this study the subjects have been performed divergence of movements on a narrow platform that is represented in MC_3.

Fluency, the component of creativity refers to a rapid flow of ideas and tendencies to change directions and modify information. In this study MC_4 represents fluency which has measured the number of times a subject hit the target with a ball.

Elaboration component refers to the expanding and combining activities of higher thought. It shows production of detailed steps, variety of implications and consequences which can be quantitatively measured. In this study MC_5 measured the elaboration component.

Thus, the researcher has taken a sincere effort to test the motor creativity of the subjects and also has taken into consideration the relatedness of creativity components and motor creativity components.

Creativity differs according to age (Yamanto, 1960; Torrance et al., 1960; Jarial, 1983) and that has been substantiated by many researchers.

Likewise creativity differs according to gender (Pandit, 1976; Beveridge, 1973; Irvin, 1976) and also according to area (Passi, 1982; Sehgal, 1978) and culture also has an influence in creativity (Rogers, 1968; Torrance, 1978).

There may have other variations in creativity according to various populations. Thus motor creativity also has to be influenced by all those varied conditions and circumstances. In addition, creative motor movements do vary according to the interest of the individuals in different forms of physical activity (Sigmundova et al., 2005), Self-concept (Justo, 2007).

There is plenty of research in the area of creativity in abroad as well as in our country aiming at finding different dimensions and influencing factors in different populations in terms of their age, gender, locality, culture and many other considerations. Studies on motor creativity are very few in number in our population or in the population of other parts of the world. Of all the studies on motor creativity very few have been published either in printed form or in electronic media.

With such background concept, this investigation has been attempted with a view to study motor creativity of the teen age students with regard to their intelligence, achievement motivation, academic achievement, age, gender and area.

1.5 Statement of the Problem

Since creativity is more innate and may also be nurtured it follows the general pattern of universality like intelligence, achievement motivation, academic achievement in having individual differences.

Age, gender and area may prove influential correlates in establishing such differences in motor creativity in particular as a part of creativity in general.

The present study has thus been designed to ascertain creative motor responses of the 13–19 years male and female students with regard to their intelligence, achievement motivation, academic achievement, age, gender and area. Thus, the study entitled "An In-depth Study on Motor Creativity in Teenage Students".

1.6 Purpose of the Study

The purpose of the study was to understand motor creativity of teenage students and to get a thorough picture on motor creativity of this population. The following purposes were selected to reach the end. The purposes were –

i) to assess motor creativity of teen age students with respect to their age;
ii) to assess gender influence, if any, on the parameters in teenage students;
iii) to assess area influence, if any, on the parameters in teenage students;
iv) to compare motor creativity of teenage students in terms of age, gender and area;
v) to predict the relationships between motor creativity and selected dependent variables i.e., intelligence, achievement motivation and academic achievement;
vi) to assess and compare motor creativity of early and late teen students in relation to gender and area;
vii) to find out the relationship between motor creativity with intelligence, achievement motivation and academic achievement in early and late teen students with reference to gender and area;
viii) to predict motor creativity as the independent variable from the dependent variables like intelligence, achievement motivation and academic achievement according to age, area and gender.

1.7 Significance of the Study

This study might prove significant in many ways. Those are as following :

1) The study may throw light on the aspect of creative motor responses of the selected age group, or of any particular age in the group concerned.
2) It may help to reveal the influence of age, if any, on intelligence and motor creativity in relation to gender and area.
3) It may reveal gender influence, if any, on motor creativity, intelligence motivation and academic achievement in relation to age and area.
4) The study may reveal the influence of age group if any on intelligence, achievement motivation, academic achievement and motor creativity in relation to gender and area.
5) It may reveal the influence of area if any on motor creativity, intelligence, achievement motivation and academic achievement in relation to gender and age.
6) The investigation may help to find out the individual differences among boys and girls, in relation to motor creativity, intelligence, academic achievement and achievement motivation.
7) From the derived correlation of the selected parameters physical educators, coaches and conscious guardians and others dealing with motor creativity may find some sort of objective guidance as to the creative applications of intelligence achievement motivation and academic achievement of students under their charge.
8) The study may reveal the latent potentialities, if any, among such a population, and help to catch them and creative application of physical working capacity may be uplifted.
9) It may help the physical educators and coaches to motivate their pupils in exhibiting creativeness in instant action situations.
10) This study may suggest for formulating training programme for development of quality and achievement of excellence.

1.8 Delimitation of the Study

1) The age group of the subjects for this study had been delimited to a range between thirteen to eighteen years. This age range covered the beginning of adolescence, its turbulent years, followed by gradual move towards stability – a period which was supposed to have a strong bearing on the selected parameters.
2) The study was conducted on five hill area schools and five plane area schools, from the hill district of Darjeeling and a plane district of Murshidabad in West Bengal.
3) The study was restricted only to the three dependent variables viz., intelligence,

achievement motivation and academic achievement for understanding the motor creativity of the selected population.
4) The samples consisted of nine hundred and sixty students – selected through systematic random sampling. Two hundred and forty were male students from hill area and two hundred and forty male students of plane area. Equal numbers of female subjects were selected from hill area as well as from the plane area.

1.9 Limitation

1) The researcher could not cover all the districts of West Bengal because of time factor and financial involvement.
2) For conducting the tests of both hill area and plane area some research scholars, some post graduate Physical Education students and some Physical Education teachers assisted the researcher. Though all of them were oriented with the whole procedure yet individual differences and human factor could not be avoided.
3) It was not possible for the part of the researcher to conduct all the tests for all the subjects on the same day as the number of subjects was large and the duration of the school hours were limited.
4) The environmental conditions of different test days although, more or less, were the same, effects of environmental conditions, if any, were beyond the control of the researcher.
5) Since motor creativity of a person also depend on many psychological factors, the researcher had no control over the unspecified psychological factors. But since no abnormality was detected in the general behaviour of the individual samples of this study, the psychological make-up of them were assumed to be normal.

1.10 Definition of Terms and Explanation of Concepts

1.10.1 Motor Creativity

An individual's motor behaviour which exhibits new ideas in executing motor skills, new techniques and new strategies to win over the situation, is influenced by the individual's creative imaginations coupled with his motor ability.

So, motor creativity is the capacity of the individual to express creatively through motor behaviour and motor movement. It is a combined expression of creative thinking and motor ability through creative motor movements in the distinct shape of individuality, originality, uniqueness, variability, etc.

1.10.2 Intelligence

Intelligence is, as P. E. Vernon (1970) says, a general innate capacity underlying all our abilities, dependent on the genes we inherit, and therefore fairly constant through life.

Intelligence is a unit responsible for gathering and interpreting information.

It is an all-round cognitive ability, said Cyril Burt. Intelligence is a complex set of qualities including –

i) the appreciation of a problem, and the direction of the mind towards its execution;

ii) the capacity for making necessary adaptations to reach a definite end; and

iii) the power of 'self criticism' to judge well, understand well, to reason well.

These are the essential activities of intelligence, said Alfred Binet.

Intelligence provides the capacity to utilize past experiences to solve new problems. According to Terman, an individual is intelligent in proportion to his ability to carry on abstract thinking.

Heim defines intelligent activities to be consisting of grasping the essentials in a given situation and responding appropriately to them.

In fine, intelligence is the aggregate or global capacity of the individual to act purposefully, to think rationally, and to deal effectively with his environment, as said by David Wechsler.

All the above definitions speak appropriately of that all-pervading quality called intelligence. Sometimes these direct towards heredity, and sometimes towards environment. Research findings show that intelligence depends on both heredity and environment, but heredity seems to play a greater role than environment. However, both heredity and environment are responsible for nurturing this amazing quality.

1.10.3 Achievement Motivation

Achievement Motivation is defined as the need to perform well, or the striving for success, and evidenced by persistence and effort in the face of difficulties.

Achievement Motivation is regarded as the central human motivation. Staying motivated keeps a person active and gives a feeling of being in control. People who are motivated by achievement often set fairly difficult but realistic targets, which ensures that they achieve their goals.

It is something that causes a person to make an effort to become successful and be goal oriented. Obviously, it is what people need to achieve a 'goal of life'.

In addition, achievement motivation also makes people work on a specific problem rather than just wait for results. This is a very positive way to handle difficult situations especially in reaching goals. To achievement motivated person, the accomplishment itself is a reward.

Achievement motivation typically refers to an individual's competence at striving to achieve goals. It is also sometimes viewed as someone's ability to select challenging yet attainable goals and then accomplish them.

It can help people accomplish their goals in their lives whether at work or in their personal life.

"Achievement motivation is what gets you going, keeps you going and determines where you are trying to go" (Salvin, 2006).

Recently several investigators adopted a multi-factorial approach to Achievement Motivation. According to this approach the domain of achievement is composed of diverse and relatively independent components.

According to Cassidy and Lynn the underlying factors of achievement motivation are dominance, competitiveness, aspiration for status.

1.10.4 Academic Achievement

Academic Achievement can be defined as excellence in all academic disciplines, in class as well as in co-curricular activities. It includes excellence in sporting behaviour, confidence, communication skills, assertiveness, arts, culture and the like.

The concept of academic achievement refers to the achievement by individuals of objectives related to various types of knowledge and skills. These objectives are socially established, based on age, prior learning and capacity of individuals with regard to education, socialization and qualification.

The factors that can hinder academic achievement are :
i) Behavioural Problems;
ii) Educational Inequalities;
iii) Educational Policy Analysis;
iv) School Dropout;
v) School-Family-Community-Partnership.

Academic Achievement is something we do or achieve at school, college or University – in class, in a laboratory, in literary or field work.

CHAPTER – II
REVIEW OF RELATED LITERATURE

A number of studies have been found on creativity in its different aspects – verbal, figural or artistic. But very few investigators, it seems, have been attracted towards the creative manifestations through motor activity. Some studies on creative dance movements are available; but studies on the various facets of motor creativity have not been noticed.

Literature on intelligence and achievement motivation although plenty, related studies on intelligence and achievement motivation in relation to motor behaviour (creativity) have not been found many in number.

However, the coverage, as presented in this chapter, has been attempted as adequate as possible under the circumstances and within the limited time, and some useful information have been extracted by pulling together relevant findings. The important ones have been noted and critically examined to draw some general conclusions to use these as references for comparison of the present study and interpretation thereon.

White (1971) investigated to ascertain a relationship between the aspects of body concept, creativity and sports proficiency. Thirty one English school boys (Sample H_1) in the 13–15 years of age range were given a half minute version of motor test items representing motor creativity and body awareness. Another thirty-one boys (Sample H_2) were given two minute version of the test items. A further sixty boys (sample SB) responded to similar test items which were scored at half a minute and at two minutes by two independent scores. The sample of H_2 with the two minute version in respect of motor creativity, body awareness and sports proficiency were all positively related. For sample SB, motor creativity was positively related to body awareness, verbal creativity and sports proficiency. Differential proficiency between open and closed skill did not distinguish between low and high groups on the major variables of movement.

Creativity studies in motor area could not be made available in plenty. Rogers (1984) wanted to find a relationship between use of unstructured and structured play materials and the variables of creativity as manifested by pre-school embedded Figures Test and Thinking Creativity in Action and Movement Test. From the results of this study it was found that almost no relationship existed between unstructured and structured play materials. There was no significant difference in the relationship of the use of unstructured and structured materials and the variables of creativeness.

Glover (1974) tried to develop a tool for measuring motor creativity of college women. The theoretical construct of the Torrance test of creative thinking (figural form) was used as the model to develop twelve movement tasks for explanatory purposes. The task consisted of three types of activities: a warm up activity with one stimulator, an activity with several stimulators and an activity with one repeated and traditional stimulation. The motor creativity test, composed of three tasks (move to sound, see and move, and hoops and lines) was administered four times to twenty five college women who were enrolled in the physical education service course program at the University of Oregon. Three judges were trained to describe, analyze and evaluate movement performances of the subjects. All the data, collected four times, were treated statistically to determine mean, standard deviation, and intercorrelation co-efficient among the task variables and the evaluation sessions. From the analysis the following conclusions were drawn:

Based upon the theoretical construct of the Torrance Test of Creative Thinking (figural form), the motor creativity, composed of three tasks, was a valid tool for measuring motor test was a valid tool, the scoring system which enables judges to describe, analyze and evaluate movement performance of the subjects, needs further refinement in order to be an objective and reliable system for evaluating motor creativity.

O'Neill (1982) tried to find out a relationship between refined movement analysis and motor creativity of grade two children. The researcher had developed a test of motor creativity but the test had been limited to notating instances of unusual and unique responses. The Refined Movement Analysis Category system and scoring procedures of Motor Creativity test were developed by the investigator. This study was conducted on 26 grade two subjects. From the data a statistically significant relationship between the scores from Refined Movement Analysis Category System and Motor Creativity Test was found. Multiple regression analysis identified direction and a combination of direction and flow as possible predictor of motor creativity. The Refined Movement Analysis Category System was found to be a valid measure of motor creativity.

In the year 1986, Le Break wanted to develop a test of motor creativity for the children from kindergarten through grade three. The Motor Creativity Test for Elementary School Children (K-3) which was designed by the investigator to measure a child's ability to create divergent movement responses to problem-solving tasks was an individually administered test consisting of five items task. Objective scoring procedures allowed for analysis of the child's movement responses. Each test was scored for fluency (number of responses) and for transformations (number of different elements the children varies with each scoring category of the test). Sum of those scores yields a total test score. The motor creativity test was administered by the investigator and two trained raters to 32 subjects including equal number of boys and girls. Pearson correlations and two-way analysis of variance procedures were utilized to determine the significance of any score deviations. One way analysis of variance and multiple regression analysis were also used for analysis.

It was concluded that (i) the motor creativity test was a reliable instrument for use with children in kindergarten and grade three; (ii) it yielded a higher validity coefficients than similar instruments for children of this age group (iii) it yielded scores which showed developmental increases (iv) it yielded scores which showed no gender differences.

Hwang (1987) in his study tried to determine the effectiveness of movement and music motivations used in a fantasy art program upon fifth grade children's creative thinking and artistic creativity. A non-equivalent control group design was used with univariate analysis of covariance to determine the effects of treatment on four creative thinking variables and two artistic creativity variables. The total subjects for the treatments in each study respectively were 52 and 38, the total subjects for cross cultural comparison of the music treatment were 66. All the subjects went through the Torrance Test for creative thinking Form–A and Form–B, and Hwang Creative Drawing Test. The results from the two studies suggested that movement and music movement in fantasy art lessons were as effective as verbal questioning in nurturing fluent and elaborative thinking. The three movements had no differential effects on artistic originality and artistic elaboration.

In the year 1980, Ramirez tried to identify certain techniques and methods used by creative movement specialists for developing creative movement programme, and to develop a unit of instruction from the results of the study in teaching creative movement skills. The opinions and identification of technique and methods were obtained by collecting information from the most recognized authorities in creative movement in U. S., based upon the findings of a survey.

Phillip (1963) in his study tried to investigate relationship between various forms of creativity, and to determine whether the expression of motor creativity was related to the selected motor skill. The test administered to the fourth grade students (N=26) consisted of creative thinking tests, a motor creativity test battery and motor skill tests. The following conclusions were drawn from the study that:

1) the expression of motor creativity through movement was not related to performance on the selected motor skill items;
2) creativity did not appear to be a generalized trait in as much as significant relationships

were not found between the various aspects of creativity;
3) a tendency towards generalization of creativity was found for girls, but not for boys;
4) a combination of weight, figural fluency and figural originality accounts for a significant amount of variability in motor creativity for boys, while a combination of figural and verbal creativity factors did the same for girls and
5) boys of this age performed significantly better than girls on skill tests involving strength, while girls excelled on balance and agility items.

Wilson (1984) worked over a four year period on university students (N= 50) enrolled in a required elementary education and physical education course focussing on creative movement experiences. The subjects went through movement therapy, improvisational dance forms including creative movement and contact improvisation. From the pre-test and post-test results the following conclusions were drawn: participants in creative movement reported awareness primarily in emotional and then in physical terms. Contact improvisation participants also reported the experiences with emphasis on emotional and then physical awareness. From the results of this study it was found that creative movement and contact improvisation experiences affected self-awareness.

Rose (1983) hypothesised that children exposed to a creative dance movement activity which integrated physical movement (creative dance movement) had a higher mean test scores than children who were exposed to non-movement activity or the regulated movement activity related to spelling instruction; and also the children using the creative dance movement approach had higher mean scores on recall at one, two and three week intervals, when compared to those of the regulated movement and non-movement groups. Collected data did not support the two hypotheses.

The study of Beveridge (1973) was concerned with relationships among motor creativity, movement satisfaction and the qualitative use of certain movement factors of second grade children. Subjects were forty five second graders who were videotaped while offering solutions to four different movement problems.

Statistical analysis of the data showed that there were sex and problem interaction effects on the responses to the motor creativity test. From the result of this study, of the four problems only one could be used, of which the scores were not affected by the gender factor.

Boys were more consistent in their responses to all four problems than were the girls. The boys and the girls did not differ significantly on their expressed movement satisfaction, motor creativity, or on their use of the movement factors involved in the study. The two motor creativity factors measured fluency and originality; they correlated very highly with one another beyond the point .001 level. This led to conclusion that one factor alone could not be scored in future administration of the test.

The purpose of Laston's (1971) study was to determine what relationships between verbal, figural and motor creativity of black and culturally deprived children. The subjects of this study were fifty students (boys-26 and girls-24) aged ten through twelve. There instruments were selected to gather the necessary data. The Torrance Test of Creative Thinking; Verbal Form-A and Figural Form–A were used to evaluate creative thinking abilities. Wyrick Test of Motor Creativity (1966) was used to evaluate motor creativity. Data were collected on twelve variables and statistical calculations were done. The following conclusions were made:

1) The motor creativity and the verbal creativity batteries assessed similar qualities to a moderate degree for the total population, and the boys and girls respectively.
2) A lack of relationship existed between verbal creativity and figural creativity for girls.
3) There were significant differences between the means of the boys' and the girls' performances in respect of verbal creativity, figural creativity and motor creativity;
4) The verbal creativity and figural creativity test batteries could be used to predict motor fluency of girls, motor originality for boys and motor creativity for the total population and boys group.

Irvin (1976) in his study compared first grade and third grade students in a program with and without physical education specialist. The students were measured on traits of motor creativity, locus of control and self-concept. It was concluded from the analysis of the data that at the third grade level, males scored significantly better than females on the motor creativity test in both schools. All the first grade level females in the physical education specialist-aided program scored significantly better than the males. So, the physical education specialist aided program did not significantly change the measures of motor creativity. The traits of motor creativity, self-concept and locus of control were quite specific with no relationship, as indicated by the data of the study.

Trigg (1978) investigated the effects of varying amounts of creative modern dance activities on subjects' creative thinking abilities and self concept. Torrance Test of Creative Thinking Figural Form-A and Figural Form-B were used to determine the effects and to what degree a significant relationship existed between creative thinking ability and self-concept.

Findings of this investigation were that the amount of creative modern dance experience had no significant effect on neither his / her creative thinking abilities nor on self-concept, and also no significant relationship existed between creative thinking ability and self-concept.

Lubin (1979) investigated the changes in motor creativity of pre-school deaf children (N = 24), three to five years old, after a four-week experimental period of guided movement exploration on a novel piece of play apparatus, the London Trestal Tree. Data were collected on motor creativity using the Torrance Test of Creativity thinking in action and movement, and the Lubin Motor Creativity Testing Protocol (derived from the Sherill Rown-Lubin adaptation of Wyrick's Motor Creativity Test).

Children were videotaped before and after the four week experimental period in trials for five minute duration while they played freely on the London Trestal Tree Apparatus. On the same day the children were exposed to the Torrance Test of Creative Thinking in action and movement.

The resulting videotapes were viewed by two experts who independently recorded the motor creativity data by making frequency of occurrence (motor frequency) and uniqueness to motor responses (motor originality) on reconstructed individual motor fluency and motor originality score sheets. High inter-rate objectivity and test-retest reliability measures were computed. Motor Creativity data from the protocol were treated by multivariate factorial of co-variance. On the basis of the findings, it was concluded that pre-school deaf children exposed to 20 days of guided movement over a control group in motor creativity measured by the Torrance Test, had observed no significant increase over a control group in motor creativity measured by the Lubin Protocol. The findings indicated the implications for teaching methodology used with pre-school deaf children.

Brennan (1976) examined the relationship among creative ability in dance, field independence-dependence, and selected attributes of creative personality. Sixty one dance majors were selected as the subjects of the study. The subjects were directed into five separate clusters, and subjected to (i) Movement Performance Test (originality, flexibility) (ii) Experts' rating, (iii) Divergent Thinking Tests (iv) Field Independence dependence measures, and (v) Movement Performance Test (fluency).

Within the limitations of the investigation the following conclusions were drawn : (i) no relationship existed among the three constructs pertinent to the study, (ii) two of the movement performance measures showed potential as valid and reliable measures of dance-creativity if further refined, (iii) the two methods of evaluating dance creativity tended to identify the same individuals as more or less creative, (iv) the more creative dancers were not more field independent than the less creative dancers, and (v) the more creative dancers were not characterised by more creative attributes than the less creative dancers.

Truhon (1982) tested the model that playfulness was evident in play that affected creativity. Kindergarteners (N = 30) were allowed ten minutes to play, and were then administered the alternate test, the figural subjects of the Torrance tests of creative thinking. Their behaviour during play were recorded and rated on the playfulness scale. The cluster analysis of these variables resulted in six clusters: Playfulness Intelligence (PI), Playfulness Fun (PF), shifts, complexity, verbal creativity and non-verbal creativity. Submission of these clusters to path analysis revealed good fit between predicted and observed correlations. Results suggested that there were two parts to the playfulness scale and that these parts reflected the cognitive and negative aspects of play.

Sharma (1987) investigated creativity on a self-developed test and studied its relationship with an intrinsic value.

Ghosh (1988) examined the relationship among creativity, motor ability and motor creativity of adolescent students. Six hundred school going students, both boys and girls of the age group 13–16 years were selected as subjects from the schools of West Bengal for this study. Within the limitations of the investigation the following conclusions were drawn:

1) Athletes were superior to non-athletes in motor creativity.
2) Male athlete group was superior in creativity, motor ability and motor creativity to all the other three groups (i.e., male non-athletes, female athletes and non-athletes).
3) Creativity of male athletes was directly related to motor ability and motor creativity.
4) Creativity of male students, gender-wise, and non-athletes, strata wise were better related to motor creativity.
5) Motor Creativity scores of male athletes, male non-athletes, female athletes and female non-athletes were directly related with motor ability scores.
6) The scores of all the four groups in motor creativity, creativity and motor ability had multiple correlations.
7) Motor creativity scores were directly related to scores in motor ability and creativity, and also dependent upon them.

Khatena (1987) reported fourteen experimental studies on training in creativity. He developed a training program which consisted of five strategies; namely - breaking away from the obvious and common place, restructuring, synthesis, transportation and analogy, with exercises that used both figural and verbal contents. This program was tried with necessary modifications on adults, college students, young children, pre-school disadvantaged students etc. In general, the strategies effectively stimulated the creative imagination to produce original verbal images. He concluded that expressing oneself creatively, generally and in original images specifically, can be enhanced with training, that this applies to young people as well as adults and that both high and low creative could benefit from such training.

Stalec et al. (2007) tried to find out the impact of dance aerobics training on the Morpho-Motor status in female high school students. The aim of this study was to analyse the impact of special programmed physical education including dance, aerobics and rhythmic gymnastics on the development of motor and functional abilities and morphological characteristics of fourth grade high school female students in Zagrsh. A total sample of 220 high school student aged 16–18 years were divided into two groups, experimental group (N= 115) students attending the program composed of dance structures and aerobics and control group (N=105) students attending classic program of physical education. A set of three morphological variables, six motor variables and one functional variable were applied in both groups in three occasions during an academic year. Two-factor analysis of variance showed the experimental program to significantly influence the development of co-ordination, agility and specific rhythm, co-ordination, functional aerobic ability, repetitive and explosive strength and flexibility, along with significant reduction of overweight and adipose tissue. The study results clearly indicated that the existing programs of physical education needed to be revised and replaced by more appropriate ones.

Sigmundova et al. (2005) investigated how conditions and educational environment change related to physical behaviour of adolescents. The aim of this study was to find and describe the possible causes of interest in adolescents in physical activity and physical education with use of qualitative analysis and to contribute to explication of other characteristics of physical behaviour. Adolescents' opinion, the level of conditions and educational environment were gathered through semi-structured interviews and their following qualitative analysis with use of a paradigmatic model of axial coding of basic proven theory. Altogether twenty seven interviews were conducted. According to adolescents the principal cause of low level of physical activity was the lack of free time. School physical education, was for most adolescents, the only source of relatively intensive exercise. Favour of school physical education depended especially on the content of the lessons, the teachers approach and the class team.

Justo (2007) tried to analyse the effects of the creative relaxation program (independent variable) on the levels of motor creativity and self-concept (dependent variable), a longitudinal quasi-experimental design was used to compare the groups using pre-test – post-test measurement with an experimental and a control group. The Thinking Creatively in Action and Movement Test by Torrance (1980) was used to assess motor creativity. To assess the variable self-concept, the Perception of Child Self Concept test was utilised.

Statistical analysis of the variables showed significant differences in favour of the experimental group with regard to the control group. The results obtained in the research work agreed with those found by other studies, thus demonstrating the feasibility of stimulating self-concept and creativity in the Infant Education stage.

Trevles (2003) examined how far fluency and flexibility in movement pattern production, as indicatory elements of divergent thinking and critical thinking were related to a variety of psychological elements (physical spontaneity, social spontaneity, cognitive spontaneity, manifest joy, sense of humour) that compositely contribute to playfulness, an internal personality characteristics. A total of two hundred and fifty preschool children participated in the study. Their teachers completed the Greek version of Children's Playfulness Scale. The Divergent Movement Ability Test was used to rate the children's motor creativity. The data indicated a significant correlation between total playfulness and – (i) motor fluency and (ii) motor flexibility. This means that playfulness and creativity were inter-connected because movement during pre-school age were the primary way of action, expression, learning and development.

Smith-Autard (2002) advocated an equal emphasis on creativity, imagination, individuality and acquisition of knowledge of theatre dance. She articulated Haynes (1987) summary of Rudolf Loban's view of creativity as personal expression – a means of evolving a style of dance which was 'true' to the individual personality and facilitated harmonisation of the individual and helped lead towards self-realisation (toward what Jung called the process of individualisation). Then, drawing on the work of Best (1985) made it clear that she saw this view of creativity as misconceived. She disagreed with the method through which this creativity might be achieved, "in the context of exploring and experimenting movement for oneself and that creativity and imagination are inborn facilities which need not be educated".

Georgios (2003) evaluated children's creativity and children's creative movement in pre-school age as for kinetic flexibility, fluency and originality. For evaluation of these specific parameters the Divergent Movement Ability Test was used. Participants were 73 children (girls–38 and boys–35). The comparison was made between pre-school children coming from the province and cities, who participated in, out of school kinetic activities at the gym. The results of the study had shown that the differences which were ascertained regarding kinetic flexibility, fluency and originality, according to the accomplishment of skilfulness and manipulation concerned only the team that took part on the organised out-of school activities at the gym. No differences were shown between sexes, in order to create different levels of approach in kinetic, flexibility, fluency and originality. Kinetic creativity observed to act as the motive of the development of a creative behaviour on kindergarten-age children. As a result they became more creative, expressive and inventive.

Marta and Carlota (2008) analyzed the diversity of motor skills related to three different kind of instruction: descriptive, metaphoric and kinetic with a special emphasis on the detection of temporal patterns (T-Patterns). Twelve undergraduates studying sport and physical education, but without experience in dance, were observed during 24 lessons of Body Movement. Using observational methodology and technology applied to movement, the aim was to adopt the observational instruments of motor skills, so as to create an instrument capable of analysing the motor skill responses generated in lessons of Body Movement and Dance. The results as reflected by the T-pattern detected show that (i) participants try to generate their own motor skills but copy some fundamental components of the instructions and (ii) the criterion of stability in two configurations (support and axial) is the predominant category. Sequential and coordinated locomotion also appears to be very relevant.

Pagona (2009) revealed in their study that creative children often have difficulty in forming their self-concept because parents may suppress their creative ideas. The purpose of the study was to investigate the relationship between motor-creativity and self-concept. Wyrik's Motor Creativity Test and the Pictorial Scale of Perceived Competence and Social Acceptance for Young Children were administered to a sample of 414 children aged from 6 ± 0.3 years to 7 ± 0.3 years. Factor analysis for the Self Concept measures revealed a 4-factor solution. The amount of variance explained most of the variance (18.2%) correlation analysis related motor creativity with the self-concept factors, and specifically with the first factor. It was observed that perceived material acceptance had a significant role in explaining children's motor creativity.

Wang (1998) investigated the effects of creative movement program on the motor creativity of Taiwanese pre-school children, hypothesizing that there would be no significant difference in motor creativity between children participating in the creative movement program and those participating in a control group. The intervention group completed a 6-week, two days per week, creative movement program which was based on

Gilbert's (1992) conceptual approach lesson plan format. The control group participated in an unstructured free setting. Pre-test and post-test data were collected using Torrance's Thinking Creatively in Action and Movement Scale, which assessed changes in the children's motor creativity. Results indicated that the experimental group had significantly higher levels of motor creativity than did the control group, suggesting that the creative movement program was essential to the development of the total child.

Now, what are the intellectual traits required for creative ability? Numerous introspective reports, written by creative persons in a variety of fields are available; but they are not particularly helpful in providing clues to the measurement of those human abilities that would enable psychologists and educators to select the potentially creative artist, scientist, mathematician, dancer, musician or author. In fact some creative individuals are quite unable to explain their mental processes, even at a descriptive level.

Philosophical and psychoanalytical theories of creativity have been expounded. One principle that seems to be widespread among these writers is that creativity does not occur in a vacuum; it occurs in areas of experience, interest and work to which the person has been 'intensively committed in his conscious living'. This trait alone is not sufficient, though it is necessary.

It is also necessary to differentiate among creative abilities in the several fields, each of which has some elements in common with the others; but each also has its own special requirements and elements.

Available psychological tests can only reveal what levels of general intellectual ability are demanded and what levels of particularized abilities are essential in each of the creative fields. In addition, improved personality inventories and projective tests might reveal which traits, if any, are essential to each field and will differentiate individuals in one type of creativity from those and will differentiate individuals in one type of creativity from those in the others. Thus far, these objectives have not probably been achieved.

Psychological testing began with efforts to devise scientific instruments for the measurement and study of individual differences in intelligence. Measurement and analysis of this complex mental process has continued to be the most important and widespread type of psychological testing.

Intelligence is general mental adaptability to new problems and new situations of life; or, otherwise stated, it is the capacity to recognize one's behaviour patterns so as to act more effectively and more appropriately in novel situations. Thus, the more intelligent person is one who can more easily and more extensively vary his behaviour as changing conditions demand; he has numerous possible responses and is capable of greater creative reorganization of behaviour; whereas the less intelligent person has fewer responses and is less creative. The more intelligent person accordingly can deal with a greater number and a greater variety of situations than the less intelligent; he is able to encompass a wider field and to expand his area of activity beyond that of the less intelligent.

The role of ability to deal with ideas and symbols, as a measure of concept formation and abstraction, is of increasing importance in tests of general ability (intelligence) as age level increases. Proportions of verbal and numerical tests, on the one hand, and non-verbal, non-numerical on the other, undergo change at different age levels. These differences are not haphazard nor are they matters of individual whim; they depend upon the purposes of the test and the test author's conception of intelligence.

Habb (1949, 1966), a Canadian psychologist, through his experimental findings and theoretical studies in the field of physiological psychology, suggested that there are two types of intelligence: intelligence-A and intelligence-B. This intelligence-A is an innate potential for the development of intellectual functions. Intelligence-A is the capacity for development a person has and is a fully innate property that amounts to the possession of a good brain and a good neural metabolism.

Intelligence-B is the functioning of a brain in which development has already gone. It is closely in accord with everyday life, understanding, insight, quickness of thought and practical judgement. The intelligence-B is not fixed because it greatly depends upon the influence of environment.

Intelligence-C according to Vernon (1970) refers to scores on intelligence tests, which should be distinguished from all-round effectiveness of a person's mental skills, i.e. Intelligence-B.

Vernon (1969) speaking in the symposium on 'Intelligence' organised by Ontario Institute for studies in education, suggested adding a fourth meaning 'constitutional intelligence'. He meant genetic equipment as affected by pre and prenatal environment or other irreversible physiological changes. There is much evidence that certain maternal diseases, heavy manual labour or stress during pregnancy, malnutrition, birth injury and anoxia may affect the infant's brain tissues, so that however good his genes and subsequent environment, he is incapable of normal intellectual development.

Cattell (1963) opined that intelligence is composed of two components which he describes as fluid (Gf) and crystallised (Gc) intelligence. Fluid intelligence represents the influence of biological factors on intellectual development and is thought to be comparable to inherited ability. Similarly, crystallised intelligence is the outcome of the skills and concepts which have become established through cultural pressure, education and experience. However, Gf and Gc are related to intelligence A and B.

The ancient Greek philosophers believed that body and mind were not separate entities but two sides of the same thing, man. Their presumptions were further strengthened by more enlightened philosophers, scientists and educationists. Rousseau considered the mind to be the 'master' and the body the 'servant' and believed that in the process of education, "if we wish to cultivate mind, we must cultivate the parts which the mind governs, namely physique". The mind has no existence without the existence of the body. Both are inseparable. It is wrong to say that athletes do not have 'brain' but 'brawn'. Sports and games, in fact strengthen the integration between body and mind.

Hall and Lindsey (1967) on this issue observed that the organism always behaves as a unified whole and not as a series of differential parts. Mind and body are not the separate entities nor does the mind consist of independent faculties or elements, and the body of dependent organs and process. The organism is a simple body-mind relationship.

Catty (1987) argued that movement is a powerful tool and for the most part constitutes a highly emotional experience in the life of children. Physical experiences are thus seldom likely to have a neutral effect upon the mind, the psyche of the maturing child. He also remarked that 'superior athletes are the scholars of their sports'.

However, Reels and Rees (1987) summarized their studies as follows :
(1) Athletes have slightly lower intelligence than non-athletes; (2) Track athletes are significantly higher in intelligence than other athletic groups (3) Baseball athletes as a group rank intellectually below all other groups.

But Crow (1973) stated that a child may be born with a high degree of potential ability to act intelligently; unless he is stimulated through learning to exercise that capacity he may appear to be relatively dull or retarded.

Rajput (1984) undertook a study of achievement in Mathematics in relation to intelligence, achievement motivation and socio-economic status and found that (i) intelligence affected the achievements of students (ii) in classroom condition the achievement of students in Mathematics was not affected by their achievement motivation (iii) the socio-economic status of the children affected the students of Mathematics.

Mehrotra (1986) conducted this study to search out the relationship between intelligence, socio-economic status, anxiety, personality adjustment and academic achievement of tenth class students for both boys and girls. His main findings were : (i) a inverse relationship between anxiety and academic achievement (ii) a positive relationship between socio-economic status of the family of the students and academic achievement and (iii) in general, girls had comparatively higher level of anxiety than the boys.

Larson (1971) revealed that studies involving the relationship of athletic participation to intellectual and emotional measurement ignored since conflicting and inconclusive results had been obtained from studies.

Furthermore, several studies reported non-significant relationships between physical fitness and intellectual achievement scores.

Physical fitness is only one component of the total fitness of the individual and which includes mental fitness, social fitness and emotional fitness. Total fitness is really a capacity for living, since the principle of body-mind unity is a sound one. It can be argued that improvement in physical fitness through the participation in physical activities will automatically augment emotional and intellectual health.

Gokhan, et. al (1977) of Istanbul found in a research work upon the Turkish children, both boys and girls, that the co-efficient of correlation between physical ability and mental development was 0.13 which was not significant.

Fleishman (1964) confirmed the relative independence of general intellectual level and physical abilities. He also showed how an infant's general ability (intelligence) could be typically evaluated in terms of his performance on early manipulative or motor tasks. But the age at which mental growth might cease depends largely on length of schooling (especially beyond 15 years), intellectual or non-intellectual type of job, and socio-cultural factors.

Regarding intelligence and age relation it had been observed that the youngster with the highest intelligence score in the class may not always be the most intelligent. A child who was two years old chronologically than a child whose intelligence is higher might actually be more intelligent in terms of ability to adjust.

It appears that vertical intellectual growth ceases after the age of eighteen years. For more intellectual person intellectual growth is more rapid and continuous for a longer time. Similarly for less intellectual person this growth is less rigid and ceases at an earlier age. Older person often test lower on certain sub-tests of intelligence tests but higher in vocabulary, opposites and disarranged sentences. Often the older persons are superior to younger persons because of their habits and background. One cannot safely make conclusive generalizations about the relationship of age to intelligence.

Lynn (1994, 1999) formulated a developmental theory of sex differences in intelligence that challenges the view that there were no sex differences in intelligence. The theory states that the boys and girls mature at different rates such as the growth of the girls accelerates at the age of about nine years and remain in advance of boys until 14–15 years. At fifteen to sixteen years the growth of girls decelerates relative to boys. As boys continue to grow their in this age the height and their mean IQ's increase than those of girls.

Lynn, et al. (2002) contended that there is a small difference favouring females from the age of approximately 9–14 years, and a difference favouring males from the age of sixteen years onwards, reaching approximately 2.4 IQ points among adults. Data to test these two theories are reported from a standardization of the Progressive Matrices on a sample of 2689 among 12-18 years in Estonia. The results confirm the Lynn theory and show a female advantage of 3.8 IQ points among 12-15 years old and a male advantage of 1.6 IQ points among 16-18 years old. Boys had a significantly larger standard deviation than girls. In early adolescence the girls outperform boys but in later adolescence boys outperform girls.

Srivastava (1974) conducted a study to find out how far academic motivation could affect the scholastic achievement, and could contribute to the production of achievement in elementary mathematics, general science, social studies and Hindi. He concluded that academic motivation influence on academic achievement.

Uguroglu (1982) conducted a study to find out the dynamic relationship of factors predicting achievement and motivation. The samples collected by her are from Chicago circle. She used a multi-dimensional motivation instrument and some other questionnaires. One of the major findings was that motivation and peer environment significantly predict mathematics achievement.

Grigoryadis (1989) conducted a study which included determination of relation between achievement scores in English as a foreign language and motivational orientation. The study revealed that the relationship between motivational orientation and language achievement scores was not significant.

Wiener (1986) made an investigation into two levels of achievement testing: knowledge and understanding. The purpose of the study was to determine whether there was any empirical psychometric reflection of a rational dichotomy of educational achievement test items, where two levels of items were knowledge (memorisation) and understanding (reasoning). The result indicated that correlation of IQ with performance in understanding was significantly greater ($P < 0.05$) than correlation of IQ with performance on knowledge. The bipolarity had been observed with respect to test item types: knowledge level items at one pole and understanding level items on the other.

Pelechano (1972) administered tests of personality, motivation, intelligence and academic achievement on female students (N = 82) with a mean age of about sixteen years. Inter-correlation between those variables and correlation with several areas of academic performance were determined. It was concluded that intelligence and personality variables are not significantly related to academic performance, while some motivational variables were related.

Margaret et al. (1979) administered a test to estimate the typical correlation between motivation and educational achievement. Motivation factors were restricted to general, academic or mathematics self-concept, locus of control and achievement motivation; achievement outcome measures included achievement and ability tests and grade point indices. For grades 1 to 12, 232 observed correlations showed a mean of 0.338 indicating 11.4 percent of the variance accounted for, in achievement by motivation. Eight variables in a regression model accounted for 39% of the variance in the magnitude of the correlations. Grade level emerged as the only significant student characteristic; motivation and achievement were more highly correlated in students in later grade.

Oudeyer et al. (2007) observed that exploratory activities seem to be intrinsically rewarding for children and crucial for the cognitive development.

CHAPTER – III
METHODOLOGY

3.1 Introduction

This study has been conducted on teenage students, their ages ranging from 13 years to 19 years. This age group is a vitally significant period in the life of the adolescents. Biologically this period in the life of the adolescents signifies puberty affected turmoil and then gradual stabilisation towards maturity.

Keeping these changes in mind, the investigator has reviewed the results of the study from the standpoint of early adolescent period (13 years to 15 years) and late adolescent period (16 years to 19 years)

An outline of the methodological framework of the present study has been described in this section as well as procedural steps involved in the specific operations planned and gone through.

As evidenced from various studies, creativity has been found to have influencing relation with intelligence, achievement motivation, academic achievement, growing age, gender dissimilarity, regional and climatic variation, etc. Since creativity ranges across a wide variety of field, creative expressions through motor performance i.e., motor creativity, would similarly be presumed to have the above as its correlates.

The undertaken study therefore focuses mainly on motor creativity as independent variable and the other parameters as correlates and dependent variables.

The investigation has been done through three separate sets of tests to conduct the present study: two written tests and one motor performance test. Two written tests were of Intelligence and Achievement Motivation while motor performance tests were for motor creativity. The Academic Achievement of the students was collected from the school marks register according to the percentage of marks obtained in the final exam by the students in the last academic session.

3.2 Subjects

The subjects of the present study were teenager school students, both boys and girls of the age group 13–19 years (13^+ years to 18^+ years). Nine hundred sixty (N = 960) school-going students of the said age category were selected as the subjects of the present study. Age of the subjects recorded from the school admission register. Age of each subject considered in completed years. Table–1 represents the detailed distribution of subjects according to age.

Table – 1 : Distribution of Subjects

Age Group	N	Area	No. of Boys	No. of Girls
13 year	160	Plane (N = 80)	40	40
		Hill (N = 80)	40	40
14 year	160	Plane (N = 80)	40	40
		Hill (N = 80)	40	40
15 year	160	Plane (N = 80)	40	40
		Hill (N = 80)	40	40
16 year	160	Plane (N = 80)	40	40
		Hill (N = 80)	40	40
17 year	160	Plane (N = 80)	40	40
		Hill (N = 80)	40	40
18 year	160	Plane (N = 80)	40	40
		Hill (N = 80)	40	40
Total	960	Plane (N = 480)	240	240
		Hill (N = 480)	240	240

At first the researcher had taken eight students of each age group from three co-educational schools of both boys and girls, 48 boys and 48 girls from each co-educational school were selected as subjects. From the boys and girls high school of hill and plane area sixteen students of each of the six age groups were selected as the subjects. So from five hill area schools and from five plane area schools 240 boys and 240 girls each from plane area and from hill area were selected randomly following systematic random sampling method.

Among the 960 (nine hundred sixty) subjects, four hundred eighty were male and four hundred eighty were female, all belonging to six different ($13^+ - 18^{+)}$) teen age groups. The 13^+ years to 15^+ years were clubbed together as the early adolescent group; similarly, 16^+ years to 18^+ years were clubbed together as the late adolescent group.

The subjects selected from five schools of the hill area and five schools of plane area– two geo-physically distinctly different areas of West Bengal, namely, the hill district of Darjeeling and a plane district of Murshidabad. Table–2 represents the sources of subjects.

Table – 2 : The Subjects selected from the Schools

Sl. No.	Area	Name of Schools	Gender	Total No. of Subjects
1	Hill	St. Alphonsus School, Kurseong	Male	48
			Female	48
2	Hill	Himalaya H. S School, Kurseong	Male	48
			Female	48
3	Hill	Green Hill High School, Kurseong	Male	48
			Female	48
4.	Hill	Victoria Boys H. S., Kurseong	Male	96
5.	Hill	Dow Hill Girls H. S., Kurseong	Female	96
		Total Number of Subjects		480
1.	Plane	Manindranagar H. S., Cossimbazar	Male	48
			Female	48
2.	Plane	Nimtala High School, Cossimbazar	Male	48
			Female	48
3	Plane	Azimgang Don Bosco High School, Azimgang	Male	48
			Female	48
4.	Plane	Balarampur H. S. School, Balarampur	Male	96
5.	Plane	Manindranagar Girls H. S., Cossimbazar	Female	96
		Total Number of Subjects		480
		Altogether		960

3.3 Criteria Measured

Etymologically, criterion means a standard of judgement, a reference point against which a decision, especially a scientific one, can be made. For any empirical study criterion measure is an important aspect on which data are obtained to predict quantitative evaluation of human behaviour.

Motor creativity or creative motor movement is a manifested form of creativity, which has many facets to understand and predict this ability across the population, according to age, gender, locality and other clustering components. Undoubtedly, like any human attribute, there must have differences in motor creativity among the human being. Prediction of any human attribute is quite difficult as each and every of the attributes is influenced by physical, behavioural and social factors. Therefore, with the purpose of predicting creative motor movements of the teen-age students thoroughly, the criterion measures set for the study were – motor creativity, intelligence, achievement motivation, academic achievement, age, gender and locality. The details of the criterion measures are given in the forthcoming paragraphs.

Creativity consists of certain components those are Originality, Flexibility, Fluency, Elaborations, Ingenious Solution to Problems (ISP), etc. (Tiwari, 1994). In this study each of the five motor creativity components corresponds to five creativity components, namely – MC_1 to originality, MC_2 to flexibility, MC_3 to ISP, MC_4 to fluency and MC_5 to elaborations. Originality component refers to the unusual ideas and suggestions for unusual applications of particular object with uncommonness or newness. In this study originality in motor creativity was measured through MC_1 where subjects had to perform the movements of the upper part of the body as many types as possible while keeping the lower part fixed.

Flexibility component measures how many distinct different ways an individual can respond to a stimulus. Flexibility in motor creativity was measured by the number of ways a subject moved (except walking) a 10-feet distance from one line to the other and back which represents MC_2.

ISP measures inventiveness of a person in a given rigid situation. In this study the subjects were asked to perform divergence of movements on a narrow platform that is represented in MC_3.

Fluency, the component of creativity refers to a rapid flow of ideas and tendencies to change directions and modify information. In this study MC_4 represents fluency which measured the number of times a subject could hit the target with a ball.

Elaboration measures the expanding and combining activities of higher thoughts that includes the detailed steps, variety of implications and consequences in movement/ movements which can be measured quantitatively. In this study MC_5 measured by the combination of variety of movements performed by a subject in four different stations.

Thus, the researcher took a sincere effort to test the motor creativity of the subjects and taken into consideration the relatedness of creativity components and motor creativity components.

3.3.1 Tools and techniques used for data collection
a) One measuring tape.
b) Two stop watches.
c) Two tennis balls.

d) One narrow bench 6-inch wide, 18 inch high and 3-feet long.
e) One mat.
f) One whistle.
g) Two sets of questionnaire scale (Intelligence and Achievement Motivation).
h) Two sets of answer sheets.
i) Score sheets for tests of Motor Creativity.
j) Score sheet for intelligence test.
k) Calcium carbonate dust for marking.

Motor Creativity

Wyrick Test of Motor Creativity (1966) redesigned and standardized by Ghosh and Bhattacharya (1988).

Intelligence

For assessing intelligence group intelligence test framed by Bhattacharya, D. (1991) was adopted.

Achievement Motivation

For Achievement Motivation, Deo-Mohan's (2002) questionnaire for Achievement Motivation Test (n-Ach) was administered for measuring attitude towards achievement in Academic and other types of activities.

Academic Achievement

The academic achievement of the subjects was recorded according to the marks register of the respective schools according to the percentage of marks obtained by the subjects in the final examination of last academic session.

3.4 Administration of the Tests for Data Collection

The test of Motor Creativity was individually administered in such a place from where no one else could see it. In a classroom all the tests of Motor Creativity were administered. Motor Creativity scores were counted in individual score sheets.

For intelligence test scores for each item was one (1). Marking was done by following all-or-none principle. There were 72 items in all, and the full mark assigned was 72. It has been assured that the test ensured content validity and construct validity. After the general instructions, before asking the students to start answering questions in each dimension of the Group Intelligence Test, examples were demonstrated by the researcher on the black-board. Then a signal was given for the start of answering the items in the dimension. The students were then asked to stop writing and attend to the direction to be given for the next dimension of the test. Thus all the dimensions of the test were gone through. At the end, the answer scripts and the questionnaire were taken back, and scoring was done accordingly.

For Academic Achievement no such test was administered. The academic achievement of the students was recorded according to the percentage of marks obtained in the annual exam by the students in the last academic session.

For Achievement Motivation the test was administered with fifty students at a time. The achievement motivation inventory of Deo-Mohan (2002) was administered to measure the achievement motivation of the subjects. This questionnaire is of the self-rating type and can be administered in a group, with 5(five) points to rate viz., Always, Frequently, Sometimes, Rarely and Never. It has no time limit.

3.5 Motor Creativity Tests

These tests were on motor activities, performance of which reflected creativity in the motor domain.

Reliability and Validity of Motor Creativity Test Battery

Motor Creativity test battery was framed with five test items. The reliability of the test was observed by the researcher both item wise and also as a whole. The reliability of the test battery was observed by adopting the test-retest procedure. Forty boys and forty girls of same age and from the same population were taken as subjects to observe the reliability of the test. Data were collected item wise on two different days by the researcher and the expert. The co-efficient of correlation found between the data collected by the researcher and the expert were 0.82 for item no. I; 0.75 for item no. II; 0.78 for item no. III; 0.88 for item no. IV; 0.67 for item no. V. The reliability of the motor creativity test score as a whole was found to be 0.92.

The validity of the Motor Creativity Test was established by collecting the opinion of the experts. The researcher sent the test battery to five different experts in this field to opine for the validity of the test battery. They were satisfied about the validity of the test battery.

3.5.1(a) Motor Creativity Test Item No. I (Originality)

Arrangement : Subjects were asked to stand in an unobstructed plane surface.

Instruction : Each subject was asked as to how many types of movement of the upper part of the body could he make while keeping lower part of the body fixed, within a time of three minutes.

An example was demonstrated so that they could understand easily.

Scoring : Each accepted movement obtained a credit mark of one. The total number of accepted responses within the allotted three minutes was recorded as the motor creativity score from this test item no. I.

3.5.1 (b) Motor Creativity Test Item No. II (Flexibility)

Arrangements : Two parallel times were drawn on the floor maintaining approximately a gap of 10-feet.

Instruction : The subject was asked regarding how many different ways, except walking (since walking was shown to the subject by the tester) could he/she move from one line to the other line within three minutes.

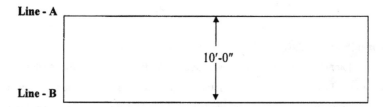

Fig. 1 : Showing the diagram of the course of test item II (Flexibility)

Scoring : Each accepted movement from one line to the other there was one mark. Total score was the total numbers of such successive accepted movements.

3.5.1(c) Motor Creativity Test Item No. III (ISP)

Arrangements : A narrow bench 6-inch was set in such a way that when the subject would stand on it he/she would not get any support from anywhere else.

Instruction : While keeping balance on a narrow base (the bench in this case), the subject was asked to perform as many new movement as he/she could do within three minutes. The movements which the subject had performed earlier would not come into the count. The subject would start and stop movement with the researchers signal.

Scoring : Total number of such new movements was counted by giving one mark for each accepted movement. Total number of such movements expressed motor creativity score from this test item.

3.5.1(d) Motor Creativity Test Item No. IV (Fluency)

Arrangement : A line AB was drawn 8-feet distant from a wall where a target 'T' was drawn.

Instruction : The subject was asked to hit the target 'T' from the line AB with a tennis ball by using any part of his/her body in as many different ways as he/she could do within three minutes.

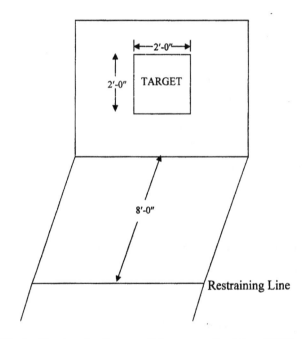

Fig. 2 : Showing the diagram of the course of test item IV (Fluency)

Scoring : Each accepted hitting scored one mark. Total number of accepted hits on the wall was the motor creativity score from this test item.

3.5.1(e) Motor Creativity Test Item No. V (Elaboration)

Arrangement : Four stations A, B, C and D were marked on a mat and instructions were given about the exercise to be performed from the particular station.

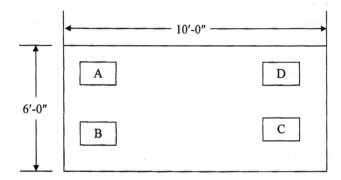

Fig. 3 : Showing the diagram of the course of test item V (Elaboration)

Station 'A' was for exercise from standing position.
Station 'B' was for exercise in sitting position.
Station 'C' was for exercise from supine position.
Station 'D' was for exercise from prone position.

Instruction : The subject was asked to perform as many exercise as he/she could do in all the stations, maintaining the stated body positions at the particular stations, within five minutes. He/she could perform any number of exercises at any particular station and devote his/her time at any station but the total time for this item should not exceed five minutes. However, after every one minute he/she was orally indicated about time.

Scoring : The accepted responses obtained from all four positions was the motor creativity score from this test.

Total Score of Motor Creativity Test :

Summation of the scores obtained from all the five test items was the total score of motor creativity.

The test-retest reliability and Motor Creativity Test Battery had been found to be 0.92 and for the validity of the tests, expert opinion had been taken by the framers of the test battery. The higher the score the higher was the motor creativity either in its components or the total score.

Fig. 4: A subject performing Motor Creativity Test Item No.I (Originality)

Fig. 5: A subject performing Motor Creativity Test Item No. II (Flexibility)

Fig. 6: A subject performing Motor Creativity Test Item No. III (ISP)

Fig. 7: A subject performing Motor Creativity Test Item No. IV (Fluency)

Fig. 8: A subject performing Motor Creativity Test Item No. V (Elaboration)

Fig. 9 : Subjects performing Written Test on Intelligence

Fig. 10 : Subjects performing Written Test on Achievement Motivation

3.6 Test of Intelligence

The test conducted with forty eight students at a time. This test was a measure of general intelligence of the subjects of the age group of 13 years to 18 years. This test was a group test. Seven dimension of measuring intelligence had been selected for the study. In the first three dimensions three types of items had been included.

1) Verbal 2) Numeral 3) Pictorial or Non-verbal

The seven dimensions were :

i) Classification ii) Analogy iii) Arrangement iv) Number Series v) Logical Selection vi) Inferences and vii) Differential Aptitude

There were 72 items under seven dimensions. The ability measures, types, number of items scheduled for each dimension had been shown in Table – 3.

Table – 3 : Format showing the Details of the Intelligence Test

	Dimensions	Types	Number of Items	Duration in Minutes
1.	Classification	a) Verbal – 8 b) Numeral – 4 c) Figural – 5	17	4
2.	Analogies	a) Verbal – 7 b) Numeral – 4 c) Figural – 6	17	4
3.	Arrangement	a) Verbal – 7 b) Numeral – 2 c) Figural – 2	11	3
4.	Number Series		8	4
5.	Logical Selection		6	2
6.	Influence		9	15
7.	Differential Aptitude		4	2

3.6.1 Scoring and Administration of Intelligence Test

Scores for each item was one (1). Marking was done by following all-or none principle. There were 72 items in all, and the full mark assigned was 72. It has been assured that the test ensured content validity and construct validity. The reliability and validity of the test have been observed by the framer of the test. The reliability co-efficient of the test was found by him to be 0.82 by test retest method. It has been worked out after intensive research on Indian population. The validity of the test was assured through the opinions of the experts obtained by him. This Intelligence Test is applicable from nine years onwards.

After the general instructions, before asking the student to start answering questions in each dimension of the Group Intelligence Test, an example was demonstrated by the researcher on the black board. Then a signal was given for the start of answering the items in the dimension. After the expiry of the schedule time for this dimension the students were asked to stop writing and attend to the directions to be given for the next dimension of the test. Thus all the dimensions of the test were gone through. At the end, the answer scripts and the questionnaire were taken back, and scoring was done accordingly.

Data thus collected have been computed in tables, analysed statistically, and interpretations made.

3.7 Test of Achievement Motivation

The test was administered with fifty students at a time. The achievement motivation questionnaire standardized by Deo-Mohan (n-Ach) was administered to measure the achievement motivation of all subjects. This questionnaire is of the self-rating type and can be administered in a group with five points to rate viz. Always, Frequently, Sometimes, Rarely and Never. It has no time limit. Fifteen factors for measuring Achievement Motivation have been selected for the study. There were 50 items out of which 13 are negative and 37 are positive items.

The fifteen factors were:
1) Academic motivation 2) Need for achievement 3) Academic challenge 4) Achievement anxiety 5) Importance of grade / marks 6) Meaningfulness of task 7) Relevance of school/college to future goals 8) Attitude towards education 9) Work methods 10) Attitude towards teacher 11) Interpersonal relation 12) Individual concern 13) General interests 14) Dramatics 15) Sports etc.

There were 50 items under fifteen factors. The ability measure factors, number of items had been shown in Table – 4.

Table – 4 : Format showing the Factors of Achievement Motivation

Sl. No	Factor	Number of Items
1.	Academic Motivation	4
2.	Need of Achievement	4
3.	Academic Challenge	4
4.	Achievement Anxiety	1
5.	Importance of grade/marks	2
6.	Meaningfulness of tasks	4
7.	Relevance of school / colleges to future goals	2
8.	Attitude towards education	4
9.	Work method	5
10.	Attitude towards teacher	3
11.	Interpersonal relations	4
12.	Individual concern	2
13.	General interest	4
14.	Dramatics	2
15.	Sports etc.	5

3.7.1 Scoring and Administration of Achievement Motivation Test

Two stencil Keys were used for scoring and for positive items and one for negative items. A positive item carries the weightages of 4, 3, 2, 1, 0 for the categories of 'Always', 'Frequently', 'Sometimes', 'Rarely' and 'Never' respectively. The negative item carries 0, 1, 2, 3, 4, and for the same categories respectively that are given above. Separate keys for positive and negative items are provided. The total score is the summation of all the positive and negative item scores.

3.8 Academic Achievement

The Academic Achievement of the student subjects (both boys and girls) of hill area and plane area, age group ranging from 13^+ years to 18^+ years taken from the school record.

3.8.1 Procedure of Data Collection

The Academic Achievement of the subjects was recorded according to the marks register of the respective schools according to the marks obtained by the subjects in the last academic session.

3.9 Design of the Study

Subjects of the study were selected from five schools of hill region and five from plane region. Academic Achievement along with the personal data like name, age and gender of each subject were recorded school wise. After that the samples were subjected to go through the tests of intelligence, achievement motivation, and motor creativity on three consecutive days. On the first two days they had gone through two written tests one for intelligence and the other for achievement motivation and on the third day the activity tests for measuring Motor Creativity were conducted.

The researcher had taken assistance from the Physical Education teachers of various schools, the trained personnel of District School Sports Association, Murshidabad and ex-research scholars of the Department of Physical Education, University of Kalyani for collecting data. For this purpose they were given a sort of orientation well in advance regarding the conduction of tests and test procedures of data collection.

3.10 Statistical Method used for the Study

After collection of data it has been statistically treated by using SPSS software version 11.5.

Mean and standard deviation (SD) were used for descriptive statistics and the data of the study are presented in the form of mean and standard deviation (SD) only.

To see the difference in Motor Creativity among the groups of six age groups of both genders from plane and hill localities, three-way ANOVA followed by Post-Hoc LSD Test was conducted.

Independent t-test was conducted to compare the groups when the subjects were classified into two groups either according to age, gender or locality (area).

Correlations among the variables were done in the form of correlation matrix to see if there is any relationship between motor creativity and all the other variables in the students of the six age groups of the study i.e., 13-year, 14-year, 15-year, 16-year, 17 years and 18-year, for hill boys, hill girls, plane boys and plane girls.

Multiple regressions were conducted to determine the level of Motor Creativity from the dependent variables which were likely to be Academic Achievement, Achievement Motivation and Intelligence in different subject categories.

CHAPTER – IV
RESULTS AND DISCUSSION

4.0 Organization

The statistical analyses of the data under Motor Creativity components and motor creativity as a whole against age, gender and area have been presented in this chapter.

The main purpose of this analysis was to find out any relationship that might exist between motor creativity and intelligence, achievement motivation, academic achievement in the perspective of the total group, late and early adolescent boys and girls group and of the boys and girls group; and also to compare the differences that might be present due to the influence of age, gender and locality.

Nine hundred sixty students were selected as the subjects of the present study. Their personal data of age, academic achievement were recorded. Among 960 students 480 were boys and 480 girls and each group of 480 consisted of 240 boys and 240 girls of hill area and 240 boys and 240 girls of plane area. In the data comparisons for both ANOVA and t-test and relationships between two variables the level of significant difference and relationship were considered to be significant at $P > 0.05$ level of confidence.

The mean and standard deviation of motor creativity and its components of 13-year age group among hill boys and girls, and plane boys, girls have been presented in Table–5. It represents the descriptive statistics in the form of mean and SD (mean ± SD) of Motor Creativity and its five components according to age, gender and area of 13-year age group. The table shows that in 13-year age group the score for plane boys (N=40) were (in mean ± SD) 20.30 ± 1.59 for MC_1, 16.45 ± 1.43 for MC_2, 14.30 ± 1.06 for MC_3, 12.35 ± 1.44 for MC_4, 21.97 ± 2.17 for MC_5, 85.30 ± 5.05 for Motor Creativity Total (MCT) and for hill boys (N = 40) the scores were 18.70 ± 1.83 for MC_1, 15.20 ± 1.69 for MC_2, 12.65 ± 1.33 for MC_3, 11.40 ± 1.41 for MC_4, 22.05 ± 2.96 for MC_5 and 80.05 ± 6.63 for MCT. In the same age group the scores (mean ± SD) for plane girls (N=40) were 19.32 ± 2.19 for MC_1, 15.65 ± 1.73 for MC_2, 14.37 ± 1.64 for MC_3, 12.97 ± 1.79 for MC_4, 21.42 ± 2.34 for MC_5 and 83.75 ± 7.61 for MCT.

Table – 5 : Descriptive statistics of Motor Creativity for 13-year age group

Gender	Area	Number	MC_1 Mean (SD)	MC_2 Mean (SD)	MC_3 Mean (SD)	MC_4 Mean (SD)	MC_5 Mean (SD)	MCT Mean (SD)
Boys	Plane	40	20.30 (1.59)	16.45 (1.43)	14.30 (1.06)	12.35 (1.44)	21.97 (2.17)	85.30 (5.05)
	Hill	40	18.70 (1.83)	15.20 (1.69)	12.65 (1.33)	11.40 (1.41)	22.05 (2.96)	80.05 (6.63)
	Total	80	19.60 (1.88)	15.82 (1.67)	13.47 (1.45)	11.87 (1.49)	22.01 (2.68)	82.67 (6.42)
Girls	Plane	40	19.32 (2.19)	15.65 (1.73)	14.37 (1.64)	12.97 (1.79)	21.42 (2.34)	83.75 (7.61)
	Hill	40	18.17 (2.61)	14.60 (2.53)	13.17 (2.87)	11.55 (2.69)	21.57 (3.75)	78.50 (9.33)
	Total	80	18.75 (2.46)	16.12 (2.21)	13.77 (2.40)	12.26 (2.38)	21.50 (3.10)	81.12 (8.36)
Total	Plane	80	19.81 (1.96)	16.05 (1.63)	14.33 (1.37)	12.66 (1.64)	21.70 (2.26)	84.52 (6.46)
	Hill	80	18.44 (2.25)	14.90 (2.15)	12.91 (2.24)	11.47 (2.14)	21.81 (3.37)	79.27 (8.08)
	Total	160	19.13 (2.22)	15.47 (1.99)	13.62 (1.98)	12.06 (1.99)	21.75 (2.86)	81.90 (7.75)

SD = Standard Deviation

Whereas, for hill girls of 13-year age group (N=40), the scores were 18.17 ± 2.61 for MC_1, 14.60 ± 2.53 for MC_2, 13.17 ± 2.87 for MC_3, 11.55 ± 2.69 for MC_4, 21.57 ± 3.75 for MC_5 and 78.50 ± 9.33 for MCT. Areawise, the MC_1 score for plane boys and girls of 13 year age group (N=80) were 19.81 ± 1.96, for MC_2 16.05 ± 1.63, for MC_3 14.33 ± 1.37, for MC_4 12.66 ± 1.64, for MC_5 21.70 ± 2.26 and for MCT the score was 84.52 ± 6.46. For hill boys and girls (N=80) the scores were 18.44 ± 2.25 for MC_1, 14.90 ± 2.15 for MC_2, 12.91 ± 2.24 for MC_3, 11.47 ± 2.14 for MC_4, 21.81 ± 3.37 for MC_5 and 79.27 ± 8.08 for MCT. For all the subjects of 13-year age group of both hill and plane area (N=160), the scores for MC_1 was 19.13 ± 2.22, for MC_2 15.47 ± 1.99, for MC_3 13.62 ± 1.98, for MC_4 12.06 ± 1.99, for MC_5 21.75 ± 2.86 and for MC Total the score was 81.96 ± 7.75.

Table – 6 : Descriptive statistics of Motor Creativity for 14-year age group

Gender	Area	Number	MC_1 Mean (SD)	MC_2 Mean (SD)	MC_3 Mean (SD)	MC_4 Mean (SD)	MC_5 Mean (SD)	MCT Mean (SD)
Boys	Plane	40	19.70 (1.96)	16.07 (1.57)	14.30 (1.60)	12.92 (1.47)	22.37 (2.67)	85.37 (8.03)
	Hill	40	19.17 (2.03)	15.22 (1.98)	13.25 (2.00)	11.60 (1.87)	23.95 (4.29)	83.20 (9.38)
	Total	80	19.43 (2.00)	16.65 (1.82)	13.77 (1.88)	12.26 (1.80)	23.16 (3.64)	84.28 (8.75)
Girls	Plane	40	19.17 (2.07)	16.07 (1.77)	13.82 (1.55)	12.60 (1.87)	22.47 (2.20)	84.22 (7.50)
	Hill	40	18.70 (2.42)	15.40 (2.99)	13.72 (2.55)	12.97 (2.54)	22.07 (4.19)	82.87 (11.10)
	Total	80	18.93 (2.25)	15.73 (2.46)	13.77 (2.09)	12.78 (2.23)	22.27 (3.33)	83.55 (9.44)
Total	Plane	80	19.43 (2.02)	16.07 (1.66)	14.06 (1.58)	12.76 (1.68)	22.42 (2.43)	84.80 (7.74)
	Hill	80	18.93 (2.23)	15.31 (2.52)	13.48 (2.29)	12.28 (2.32)	23.01 (4.32)	83.03 (10.21)
	Total	160	19.18 (2.14)	15.69 (2.16)	13.77 (1.98)	12.52 (2.04)	22.72 (3.50)	83.91 (9.08)

SD = Standard Deviation

Table-6 shows that in 14-year age group, the scores for plane boys were 19.70 ± 1.96 for MC_1, 16.07 ± 1.57 for MC_2, 14.30 ± 1.60 for MC_3, 12.92 ± 1.47 for MC_4, 22.37 ± 2.67 for MC_5 and 85.37 ± 8.03 for MCT. For hill boys of the same age group the scores were 19.17 ± 2.03 for MC_1, 15.22 ± 1.98 for MC_2, 13.25 ± 2.00 for MC_3, 11.60 ± 1.87 for MC_4, 23.95 ± 4.29 for MC_5 and 83.20 ± 9.38 for MCT. The scores of the plane girls of 14-year age group were 19.17 ± 2.07 for MC_1, 16.07 ± 1.77 for MC_2, 13.82 ± 1.55 for MC_3, 12.60 ± 1.87 for MC_4, 22.47 ± 2.20 for MC_5 and 84.22 ± 7.50 for MCT. For hill girls of the same age group the scores were 18.70 ± 2.42 for MC_1, 15.40 ± 2.99 for MC_2, 13.72 ± 2.55 for MC_3, 12.97 ± 2.54 for MC_4, 22.07 ± 4.19 for MC_5, 82.87 ± 11.10 for MCT. Areawise, the MC_1 score for plane subjects (boys + girls) of 14-year age group were 19.43 ± 2.02, for MC_2 16.07 ± 1.66, for MC_3 14.06 ± 1.58, for MC_4 12.76 ± 1.68, for MC_5 22.42 ± 2.43 and for MCT 84.80 ±

7.74. For hill subjects (boys + girls) the scores for MC_1 were 18.93 ± 2.23, for MC_2 15.31 ± 2.52, for MC_3 13.48 ± 2.29, for MC_4 12.28 ± 2.32, for MC_5 23.01 ± 4.32 and for MCT 83.03 ± 10.21. For 14 year subjects of both hill area and plane are the MC_1 score was 19.18 ± 2.14, MC_2 score 15.69 ± 2.16, MC_3 score 13.77 ± 1.98, MC_4 score 12.52 ± 2.04, MC_5 score 22.72 ± 3.50 and for MCT the score was 83.91 ± 9.08.

Table – 7 : Descriptive statistics of Motor Creativity for 15-year age group

Gender	Area	Number	MC_1 Mean (SD)	MC_2 Mean (SD)	MC_3 Mean (SD)	MC_4 Mean (SD)	MC_5 Mean (SD)	MCT Mean (SD)
Boys	Plane	40	19.72 (1.66)	17.12 (1.47)	14.67 (1.89)	13.60 (1.85)	27.62 (3.09)	92.75 (6.97)
	Hill	40	20.00 (1.56)	15.85 (1.83)	13.62 (1.86)	12.77 (1.96)	25.02 (3.46)	87.27 (6.22)
	Total	80	19.86 (1.61)	16.48 (1.77)	14.15 (1.94)	13.18 (1.94)	26.32 (3.51)	90.01 (7.12)
Girls	Plane	40	19.00 (1.97)	14.72 (1.98)	14.45 (2.08)	14.35 (1.29)	23.40 (2.77)	86.15 (6.28)
	Hill	40	19.27 (2.07)	15.95 (2.18)	14.80 (1.80)	14.20 (1.41)	25.07 (3.05)	89.52 (7.47)
	Total	80	19.13 (2.01)	15.33 (2.16)	14.62 (1.94)	14.27 (1.34)	24.23 (3.01)	87.83 (7.07)
Total	Plane	80	19.36 (1.85)	15.92 (2.11)	14.56 (1.98)	13.97 (1.63)	25.51 (3.61)	89.45 (7.38)
	Hill	80	19.64 (1.86)	15.90 (2.00)	14.21 (1.91)	13.48 (1.84)	25.05 (3.24)	88.40 (6.92)
	Total	160	19.50 (1.85)	15.91 (2.05)	14.38 (1.95)	13.73 (1.75)	25.28 (3.43)	88.82 (7.15)

SD = Standard Deviation

Table–7 represents the results of 15-year age group subjects. The scores of plane boys for MC_1 were 19.72 ± 1.66, for MC_2 - 17.12 ± 1.47, for MC_3 - 14.67 ± 1.89, for MC_4 - 13.60 ± 1.85, for MC_5 - 27.62 ± 3.09 and for MCT - 92.75 ± 6.97. For hill boys of the same age group MC_1 score was 20.00 ± 1.56, MC_2 - 15.85 ± 1.83, MC_3 - 13.62 ± 1.86, MC_4 - 12.77 ± 1.96, MC_5 - 25.02 ± 3.46 and for MCT - 87.27 ± 6.22. Whereas, for plane girls the scores were 19.00 ± 1.97 for MC_1, 14.72 ± 1.98 for MC_2, 14.45 ± 2.08 for MC_3, 14.35 ± 1.29 for

MC_4, 23.40 ± 2.77 for MC_5 and 86.15 ± 6.28 for MCT and for hill girls of 15-year age group the scores were 19.27 ± 2.07 for MC_1, 15.95 ± 2.18 for MC_2, 14.80 ± 1.80 for MC_3, 14.20 ± 1.41 for MC_4, 25.07 ± 3.05 for MC_5 and 89.52 ± 7.47 for MCT. Areawise, the MC_1 score for plane subjects (boys + girls) of 15 year were 19.36 ± 1.85 for MC_1, 15.92 ± 2.11 for MC_2 14.56 ± 1.98 for MC_3, 13.97 ± 1.63 for MC_4, 25.51 ± 3.61 for MC_5 and 89.45 ± 7.38 for MCT. For hill boys and girls of the same age group, the scores of MC_1 - 19.64 ± 1.86, for MC_2 - 15.90 ± 2.00, for MC_3 - 14.21 ± 1.91, for MC_4 - 13.48 ± 1.84, for MC_5 -25.05 ± 3.24 and 88.40 ± 6.92 for MCT. For 15-year subjects of both hill area and plane area the scores were 19.50 ± 1.85 for MC_1, 15.91 ± 2.05 for MC_2, 14.38 ± 1.95 for MC_3, 13.73 ± 1.75 for MC_4, 25.28 ± 3.43 for MC_5 and 88.82 ± 7.15 for MCT.

Table – 8 : Descriptive statistics of Motor Creativity for 16-years age group

Gender	Area	Number	MC_1 Mean (SD)	MC_2 Mean (SD)	MC_3 Mean (SD)	MC_4 Mean (SD)	MC_5 Mean (SD)	MCT Mean (SD)
Boys	Plane	40	20.32 (1.70)	16.15 (1.64)	14.70 (1.85)	12.32 (1.47)	31.20 (4.47)	95.65 (6.62)
	Hill	40	19.77 (1.88)	15.70 (2.15)	13.52 (2.01)	12.35 (1.91)	29.65 (4.30)	91.25 (7.71)
	Total	80	20.05 (1.80)	15.92 (1.91)	14.11 (2.01)	12.83 (1.76)	30.42 (4.43)	93.45 (7.47)
Girls	Plane	40	18.10 (1.62)	15.25 (1.46)	14.12 (1.48)	13.55 (1.61)	22.17 (2.79)	83.22 (6.80)
	Hill	40	17.42 (2.15)	14.72 (1.99)	13.52 (1.66)	14.40 (1.76)	25.20 (4.08)	85.27 (7.64)
	Total	80	17.76 (1.93)	14.98 (1.76)	13.82 (1.59)	13.97 (1.73)	23.68 (3.79)	84.25 (7.26)
Total	Plane	80	19.21 (1.99)	15.70 (1.61)	14.41 (1.69)	13.43 (1.54)	26.68 (5.86)	89.43 (9.14)
	Hill	80	18.60 (2.33)	15.21 (2.12)	13.52 (1.83)	13.37 (2.10)	27.42 (4.73)	88.26 (8.20)
	Total	160	18.90 (2.18)	15.45 (1.89)	13.96 (1.81)	13.40 (1.83)	27.05 (5.32)	88.85 (8.67)

SD = Standard Deviation

Table–8 represents the statistics of the 16-year age group. The scores for plane boys were 20.32 ± 1.70 for MC_1, 16.15 ± 1.64 for MC_2, 14.70 ± 1.85 for MC_3, 12.32 ± 1.47 for MC_4, 31.20 ± 4.47 for MC_5 and 95.65 ± 6.62 for MCT and for hill boys the scores were 19.77 ± 1.88 for MC_1, 15.70 ± 2.15 for MC_2, 13.52 ± 2.01 for MC_3, 12.35 ± 1.91 for MC_4, 29.65 ± 4.30 for MC_5 and 91.25 ± 7.71 for MCT. In the same age group the scores for plane girls were 18.10 ± 1.62 for MC_1, 15.25 ± 1.46 for MC_2, 14.12 ± 1.48 for MC_3, 13.55 ± 1.61 for MC_4, 22.17 ± 2.79 for MC_5 and 83.22 ± 6.80 for MC Total. Whereas, for hill girls of 16 years the scores were 17.42 ± 2.15 for MC_1, 14.72 ± 1.99 for MC_2, 13.52 ± 1.66 for MC_3, 14.40 ± 1.76 for MC_4, 25.20 ± 4.08 for MC_5, 85.27 ± 7.64 for MCT. Areawise, the MC_1 score for plane boys and girls of 16 years were 19.21 ± 1.99, 15.70 ± 1.61 for MC_2, 14.41 ± 1.69 for MC_3, 13.43 ± 1.54 for MC_4, 26.68 ± 5.86 for MC_5 and 89.43 ± 9.14 for MCT. For hill boys and girls, the MC_1 score was 18.60 ± 2.33, 15.21 ± 2.12 for MC_2, 13.52 ± 1.83 for MC_3, 13.37 ± 2.10 for MC_4, 27.42 ± 4.73 for MC_5 and 88.26 ± 8.20 for MCT. For 16 years subjects of both plane and hill area the MC_1 scores were 18.90 ± 2.18, MC_2 scores were 15.45 ± 1.89, MC_3 scores were 13.96 ± 1.81, MC_4 scores were 13.40 ± 1.83, MC_5 scores were 27.05 ± 5.32 and 88.85 ± 8.67 for MCT.

Table–9 contains the results for 17-year age group. The scores for plane boys were 20.70 ± 2.11 for MC_1, 17.82 ± 1.56 for MC_2, 14.80 ± 1.45 for MC_3, 13.92 ± 1.40 for MC_4, 23.42 ± 2.43 for MC_5 and 90.90 ± 6.06 for MCT and for hill boys the scores were 20.70 ± 2.11 for MC_1, 17.82 ± 1.56 for MC_2, 14.87 ± 1.43 for MC_3, 13.62 ± 1.97 for MC_4, 23.67 ± 1.75 for MC_5 and 91.15 ± 6.02 for MCT. In the same age group the scores for plane girls were 18.67 ± 1.74 for MC_1, 16.02 ± 1.34 for MC_2, 13.90 ± 1.31 for MC_3, 13.47 ± 1.35 for MC_4, 22.35 ± 1.86 for MC_5 and 84.50 ± 5.18 for MCT and for hill girls the scores were 20.02 ± 2.23 for MC_1, 16.12 ± 1.71 for MC_2, 15.27 ± 1.92 for MC_3, 14.60 ± 2.42 for MC_4, 26.25 ± 4.73 for MC_5 and 92.02 ± 6.44 for MCT. Areawise, the score of MC_1 for plane subjects (boys and girls) of 17-year were 19.68 ± 2.17, for MC_2 16.92 ± 1.71, for MC_3 14.35 ± 1.45, for MC_4 13.70 ± 1.39, for MC_5 22.88 ± 2.22 and for MCT the score was 87.70 ± 6.46. The hill subjects' scores were 20.36 ± 2.18, 16.98 ± 1.84 for MC_2, 15.07 ± 1.69 for MC_3, 14.11 ± 2.25 for MC_4, 24.96 ± 3.78 for MC_5 and 91.58 ± 6.21 for MCT. For 17-year subjects of both hill and plane area were 20.02 ± 2.20 for MC_1, 16.95 ± 1.77 for MC_2, 14.71 ± 1.61 for MC_3, 13.90 ± 1.87 for MC_4, 23.92 ± 3.26 for MC_5 and 89.64 ± 6.61 for MCT.

Table – 9 : Descriptive statistics of Motor Creativity for 17-year age group

Gender	Area	Number	MC_1 Mean (SD)	MC_2 Mean (SD)	MC_3 Mean (SD)	MC_4 Mean (SD)	MC_5 Mean (SD)	MCT Mean (SD)
Boys	Plane	40	20.70 (2.11)	17.82 (1.56)	14.80 (1.45)	13.92 (1.40)	23.42 (2.43)	90.90 (6.06)
	Hill	40	20.70 (2.11)	17.82 (1.56)	14.87 (1.43)	13.62 (1.97)	23.67 (1.75)	91.15 (6.02)
	Total	80	20.70 (2.10)	17.82 (1.56)	14.83 (1.43)	13.77 (1.70)	23.55 (2.11)	91.02 (6.00)
Girls	Plane	40	18.67 (1.74)	16.02 (1.34)	13.90 (1.31)	13.47 (1.35)	22.35 (1.86)	84.50 (5.18)
	Hill	40	20.02 (2.23)	16.12 (1.71)	15.27 (1.92)	14.60 (2.42)	26.25 (4.73)	92.02 (6.44)
	Total	80	19.35 (2.10)	16.07 (1.58)	14.58 (1.77)	14.03 (2.03)	24.30 (4.07)	88.26 (6.93)
Total	Plane	80	19.68 (2.17)	16.92 (1.71)	14.35 (1.45)	13.70 (1.39)	22.88 (2.22)	87.70 (6.46)
	Hill	80	20.36 (2.18)	16.98 (1.84)	15.07 (1.69)	14.11 (2.25)	24.96 (3.78)	91.58 (6.21)
	Total	160	20.02 (2.20)	16.95 (1.77)	14.71 (1.61)	13.90 (1.87)	23.92 (3.26)	89.64 (6.61)

SD = Standard Deviation

Table–10 represents the descriptive statistics of Motor Creativity for 18-year age group. In this group the scores for plane boys were 21.27 ± 1.92 for MC_1, 20.00 ± 2.20 for MC_2, 17.37 ± 1.39 for MC_3, 15.42 ± 1.35 for MC_4, 25.00 ± 1.60 for MC_5 and 98.07 ± 6.40 for MCT. For hill boys, the scores were 21.67 ± 1.49 for MC_1, 18.70 ± 1.55 for MC_2, 17.72 ± 1.50 for MC_3, 18.12 ± 1.78 for MC_4, 25.37 ± 1.76 for MC_5, 101.72 ± 5.54 for MCT. For plane girls of 18 years age group the scores were 19.20 ± 1.48 for MC_1, 16.67 ± 1.57 for MC_2, 14.62 ± 1.51 for MC_3, 13.00 ± 1.21 for MC_4, 22.15 ± 1.84 for MC_5 and 85.62 ± 5.84 for MCT. For hill girls of the same age groups the scores were 19.10 ± 1.85 for MC_1, 15.77 ± 1.65 for MC_2, 15.15 ± 2.43 for MC_3, 16.42 ± 2.63 for MC_4, 22.72 ± 3.50 for MC_5 and 89.30 ± 7.04 for MCT. Areawise, the MC_1 score for plane boys and girls of 18-years were 20.23 ± 2.00, 18.33 ± 2.53 for MC_2, 16.00 ± 2.00 for MC_3, 14.21 ± 1.76 for MC_4, 23.57 ± 2.23 for MC_5 and 91.85 ± 8.73 for MCT.

Table – 10 : Descriptive statistics of Motor Creativity for 18-year age group

Gender	Area	Number	MC_1 Mean (SD)	MC_2 Mean (SD)	MC_3 Mean (SD)	MC_4 Mean (SD)	MC_5 Mean (SD)	MCT Mean (SD)
Boys	Plane	40	21.27 (1.92)	20.00 (2.20)	17.37 (1.39)	15.42 (1.35)	25.00 (1.60)	98.07 (6.40)
	Hill	40	21.67 (1.49)	18.70 (1.55)	17.72 (1.50)	18.12 (1.78)	25.37 (1.76)	101.72 (5.54)
	Total	80	21.47 (1.72)	19.35 (2.00)	17.55 (1.44)	16.77 (2.08)	25.18 (1.68)	99.90 (8.22)
Girls	Plane	40	19.20 (1.48)	16.67 (1.57)	14.62 (1.51)	13.00 (1.21)	22.15 (1.84)	85.62 (5.84)
	Hill	40	19.10 (1.85)	15.77 (1.65)	15.15 (2.43)	16.42 (2.63)	22.72 (3.50)	89.30 (7.04)
	Total	80	19.15 (1.66)	16.22 (1.66)	14.88 (2.03)	14.71 (2.66)	22.43 (2.79)	87.46 (6.69)
Total	Plane	80	20.23 (2.00)	18.33 (2.53)	16.00 (2.00)	14.21 (1.76)	23.57 (2.23)	91.85 (8.73)
	Hill	80	20.38 (2.11)	17.23 (2.17)	16.43 (2.39)	17.27 (2.39)	24.05 (3.06)	95.51 (8.87)
	Total	160	20.31 (2.05)	17.78 (2.41)	16.21 (2.20)	15.74 (2.59)	23.81 (2.68)	93.68 (8.96)

SD = Standard Deviation.

The MC_1 score for hill boys and girls were 20.38 ± 2.11, 17.23 ± 2.17 for MC_2, 16.43 ± 2.39 for MC_3, 17.27 ± 2.39 for MC_4, 20.05 ± 3.06 for MC_5 and 95.51 ± 8.87 for MCT. For 18-year subjects of both plane and hill area, the MC_1 score were 20.31 ± 2.05, MC_2 score were 17.78 ± 2.41, MC_3 score were 16.21 ± 2.20, MC_4 score were 15.74 ± 2.59, MC_5 score were 23.81 ± 2.68 and 93.68 ± 8.96 were the score of MCT.

The overall picture of tables presents steady and gradually increasing values of all the motor creativity components, except in 16-year group and 17 / 18-year group where the steady trend of increase is broken. The reason may be that at 16-year there occurs a transition from the early adolescent age to late adolescent stage (transition from a stage of surge in physical behaviour to a rather stabilizing stage) consequent upon which the disturbance is observed. Thereafter, the steady increase in values continues, except in case of MC_5 values at seventeen years and eighteen years where there has occurred drop in increase. This sort of different findings might have occurred again due to another transition from stabilizing late adolescent to stabilized adulthood stage.

Table – 11 : Descriptive statistics of Motor Creativity for Boys and Girls Group

Gender	Area	Number	MC_1 Mean (SD)	MC_2 Mean (SD)	MC_3 Mean (SD)	MC_4 Mean (SD)	MC_5 Mean (SD)	MCT Mean (SD)
Boys	Plane	240	20.33 (1.89)	17.27 (2.14)	15.02 (1.88)	13.59 (1.77)	25.26 (4.33)	91.34 (8.10)
	Hill	240	20.00 (2.06)	16.41 (2.24)	14.27 (2.39)	13.31 (2.91)	24.95 (4.00)	89.10 (9.83)
Girls	Plane	240	18.91 (1.89)	15.73 (1.75)	14.21 (1.62)	13.32 (1.62)	22.32 (2.38)	84.57 (6.60)
	Hill	240	18.78 (2.36)	15.42 (2.28)	14.27 (2.37)	14.02 (2.72)	22.81 (4.26)	86.25 (9.43)
Total	Plane	480	19.62 (2.92)	16.50 (2.10)	14.62 (1.80)	13.45 (1.70)	23.79 (3.79)	87.96 (8.12)
	Hill	480	19.39 (2.30)	15.92 (2.31)	14.27 (2.38)	13.66 (2.84)	24.38 (4.17)	87.67 (9.73)
	Total	960	19.40 (2.16)	16.21 (2.22)	14.44 (2.11)	13.56 (2.34)	24.09 (3.99)	87.81 (8.95)

SD = Standard Deviation

Table-11 represents the descriptive statistics of Motor Creativity and its components on Boys and Girls groups. For total boys of plane area (N = 240) the scores (mean ± SD) for MC_1 was 20.33 ± 1.89, for MC_2 - 17.27 ± 2.14, for MC_3 - 15.02 ± 1.88, for MC_4 - 13.59 ± 1.77 for MC_5 - 25.26 ± 4.33 and for MCT - 91.34 ± 8.10. For total hill boys (N = 240) the scores were 20.00 ± 2.06 for MC_1, 16.41 ± 2.24 for MC_2 14.27 ± 2.39 for MC_3, 13.31 ± 2.91 for MC_4, 24.95 ± 4.00 for MC_5 and 89.10 ± 9.83 for MCT. Whereas, for total girls of the plane area (N = 240), the scores were 18.91 ± 1.89 for MC_1, 15.73 ± 1.75 for MC_2, 14.21 ± 1.62 for MC_3, 13.32 ± 1.62 for MC_4, 22.32 ± 2.38 for MC_5, 84.57 ± 6.60 for MC Total. For hill girls (N = 240) of all age groups the scores were 18.78 ± 2.36 for MC_1, 15.42 ± 2.28 for MC_2, 14.27 ± 2.37 for MC_3, 14.02 ± 2.72 for MC_4, 22.81 ± 4.26 for MC_5 and 86.25 ± 9.43 for MCT. For total boys and girls of the plane area (N = 480), the score of MC_1 was 19.62 ± 2.92, for MC_2 16.50 ± 2.10, for MC_3 14.62 ± 1.80, for MC_4 13.45 ± 1.70, for MC_5 23.79 ± 3.79 and for MCT the scores was 87.96 ± 8.12. For total boys and girls of hill area (N = 480), the scores were 19.39 ± 2.30 for MC_1, 15.92 ± 2.3` for MC_2, 14.27 ± 2.38 for MC_3, 13.66 ± 2.84 for MC_4, 24.38 ± 4.17 for MC_5 and 87.67 ± 9.73 for MCT. For all the boys and girls of the six age groups of both hill and plane area (N = N), the score was 19.40 ± 2.16 for MC_1, 16.21 ± 2.22 for MC_2, 14.44 ± 2.11 for MC_3, 13.56 ± 2.34 for MC_4 , 24.09 ± 3.99 for MC_5 and the score for MCT was 87.81 ± 8.95.

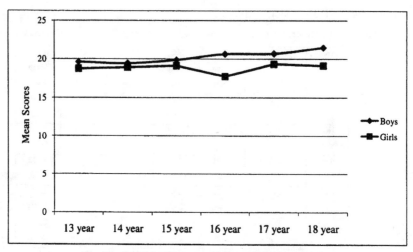

Fig. 11 : Graphical Representation of MC_1 (Originality)

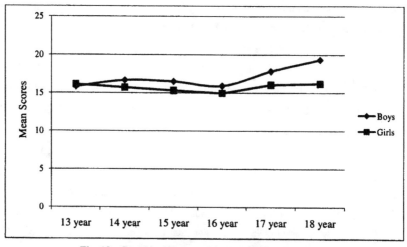

Fig. 12 : Graphical Representation of MC_2 (Flexibility)

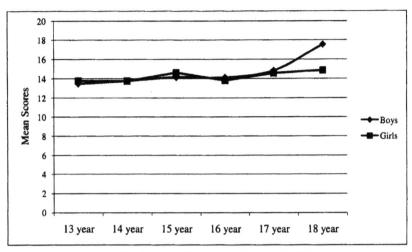

Fig. 13 : Graphical Representation of MC_3 (ISP)

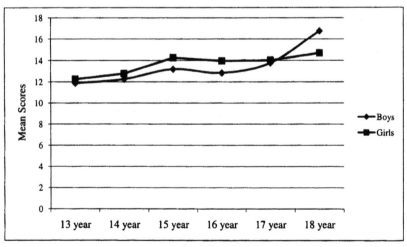

Fig. 14 : Graphical Representation of MC_4 (Fluency)

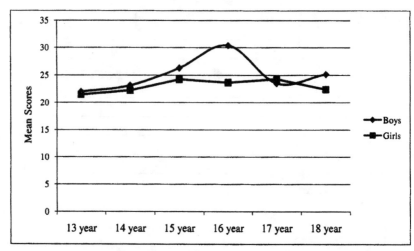

Fig. 15 : Graphical Representation of MC$_5$ (Elaboration)

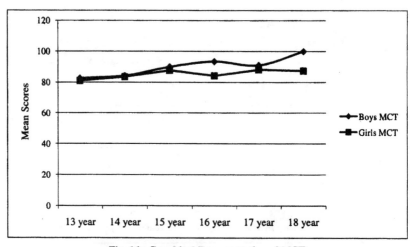

Fig. 16 : Graphical Representation of MCT

The graphical representations of Motor Creativity and its five components for both genders are presented from Fig. 11 to Fig. 16. The progression in each variable according to age is clearly understood from those figures.

Motor Creativity of teenage students in accordance with their age, gender and locality in total motor creativity as well as its five components have been calculated with the help of three-way ANOVA calculations and the results are described in the subsequent paragraphs.

Table – 12 : Three-way ANOVA on MC_1 (Flexibility)

Source of Variations	df	SS	MSS	Calculated F-value	Tabulated F-Value
Age (A)	6 - 1 = 5	244.172	48.834	12.825*	2.22$F_{0.05}$ (5,936)
Gender (G)	2 - 1 = 1	420.026	420.026	110.308*	3.85 $F_{0.05}$ (1,936)
Area (L)	2 - 1 = 1	12.834	12.834	3.371	3.85 $F_{0.05}$ (1,936)
Interaction$_1$ (A × G)	(6-1) (2-1) = 5	131.930	26.386	6.930*	2.22$F_{0.05}$ (5,936)
Interaction$_2$ (G × L)	(2-1) (2-1) = 1	2.501	2.601	0.657	3.85 $F_{0.05}$ (1,936)
Interaction$_3$ (A × L)	(6-1)(2-1) = 5	109.947	21.989	5.775*	2.22$F_{0.05}$ (5,936)
Interaction$_4$ (A×G×L)	(6-1)(2-1)(2-1) = 5	20.436	4.086	1.073	2.22$F_{0.05}$ (5,936)
Error	N – (A×G×L)= 936	20.430	3.808		
Total	960	3564.075			

Significant at 0.05 level of significance

Table-12 represents the results of three-way ANOVA of MC_1. When age was considered as the source of variation the calculated F-value of the six age groups was 12.825 was greater than (P>0.05) the tabulated F-value ($F_{0.05}$5,936=2.22). Therefore, when age is considered as a variable, significant difference is observed in MC_1 (originality) among the six age groups of the study. When gender was considered as the source of variation the calculated F-value was 110.308, which was higher than the F-critical at 0.05 level, ($F_{0.05}$1,936=3.85). Hence, a significant difference between boys and girls is found in MC_1. When area was considered as the source of variation the calculated F-value 3.371 for area was less than the tabulated F-value of 3.85, which indicates there was no influence of area on MC_1 among the teenage students.

In case of interaction$_1$ (Age × Gender) the calculated F-value 6.93 was more than the tabulated value ($F_{0.05}$5,936 = 2.22), which signifies that there is a significant difference, where age and gender both were considered as the source of variation together.

In case of Interaction$_2$ (Gender × Area) the calculated F-value (0.657) was less than the tabulated F-value (3.85) which shows no difference when gender and area both were considered as the source of variation together.

In Interaction$_3$ (Age × Area), where the source of variation were age and locality, the F-value 5.775 is greater than tabulated F-value ($F_{0.05}$5, 936 = 2.22), which reveals the notion that there is a significant difference when age and area on MC$_1$ were considered mutually.

In Interaction$_4$, when age, gender and area, all the three sources of variations were considered in combination, the calculated F-value (0.73) was less than the tabulated F-value, which indicates that there was no significant difference among the six age groups on MC$_1$ in this respect.

Table – 13 : Pairwise comparison among Group Means of MC$_1$ (Originality)

Group Means						Mean Difference	S. Error	t-value
13-Yrs.	14-Yrs.	15-Yrs.	16-Yrs.	17-Yrs.	18-Yrs			
19.125				20.03		0.90	0.218	4.13*
19.13					20.31	1.187	0.218	5.44*
	19.19			20.03		0.838	0.218	3.84*
	19.19				20.31	1.125	0.218	5.16*
		19.50	18.91			0.594	0.218	2.72*
		19.50		20.03		0.525	0.218	2.41*
		19.50			20.31	0.812	0.218	3.72*
			18.91	20.03		1.119	0.218	5.13*
			18.91		20.31	1.406	0.218	6.45*

*Significant at 0.05 level, $t_{0.05}$ (78) = 1.97

Table-13 representing only the comparisons between two age group means (mean difference) that was found to be significantly different (t-value greater than to be significant at 05 level of confidence) among the six age group means of MC$_1$.

Table – 14 : Three-way ANOVA on MC$_2$ (Flexibility)

Source of Variations	df	SS	MSS	Calculated F-value	Tabulated F-Value
Age (A)	6 - 1 = 5	719.912	143.982	41.795*	2.22$F_{0.05}$ (5,936)
Gender (G)	2 - 1 = 1	382.537	382.537	111.042*	3.85 $F_{0.05}$ (1,936)
Area (L)	2 - 1 = 1	80.504	80.504	23.369*	3.85 $F_{0.05}$ (1,936)
Interaction$_1$ (A × G)	(6-1)(2-1) = 5	238.550	47.710	13.84*	2.22$F_{0.05}$ (5,936)
Interaction$_2$ (G × L)	(2-1)(2-1) = 1	18.15	18.150	5.269*	3.85 $F_{0.05}$ (1,936)
Interaction$_3$ (A × L)	(6-1)(2-1) = 5	53.683	10.737	3.117	2.22$F_{0.05}$ (5,936)
Interaction$_4$(A×G×L)	(6-1)(2-1)(2-1) = 5	46.812	9.362	2.718*	2.22$F_{0.05}$ (5,936)
Error	N –(A×G×L)=936	3224.500	3.445		
Total	960	257096.000			

*Significant at 0.05 level of significance

In pair-wise comparisons, the mean differences were significant between 13-year and 17-year (0.90), 13-year and 18-year (1.187), 14-year and 17-year (0.838), 14-year and 18-year (1.125), 15-year and 16-year (0.594), 15-year and 17-year (0.525), 15-year and 18-year (0.812), 16-year and 17-year (1.119) and 16-year to 18-year (1.406) groups.

Table-14 reveals the three-way ANOVA of MC_2. When age was considered as the source of variation in MC_2 the calculated F-value 41.795, which was significant at 0.05 level of significance ($F_{0.05}$ 5,936=2.22). So, a significant difference was found among the six age groups of the study in MC_2. When gender was the source of variation the calculated F-value 111.042 was higher than the tabulated value ($F_{0.05}$ 1,936=3.85). Hence, in MC_2 a significant difference between boys and girls are found. When area as the source of variation, the calculated F-value 23.369 was more than the tabulated F-value ($F_{0.05}$ 1,936=3.85), which indicates that area influence in MC_2 difference among the teenage students.

In Interaction$_1$ (Age × Gender) the calculated F-value (13.84) was more than the tabulated F-value (2.22), which reveals that a significant difference is there when age and gender both were the source of variation.

In case of Interaction$_2$ (Gender × Area) the calculated F-value (5.269) was more than the tabulated F-value (3.85), which shows significant difference where gender and area both were considered as the source of variation together.

In Interaction$_3$ (Age × Area) the calculated F-value (3.117) was greater than the tabulated F-value (2.22), which reveals that there is a significant difference between age and area on MC_2 when both age and area are considered as the source of variation.

Whereas in Interaction$_4$ where age, gender, area were considered in combination, the calculated F-value (2.718) was higher than the tabulated F-value ($F_{0.05}$5,936=2.22), which reflects that there was a significant difference among the groups in MC_2 in this respect.

Table-15 reveals the comparisons between two age group means, which is found to be significantly different ($P < 0.05$) in all age groups except between 13-year and 14-year and between 17-year and 18-year age groups.

In pairwise comparisons, mean differences were significant between 13-year and 15-year (0.438), 13-year and 17- year (1.475), 13-year and 18-year (2.312),14-year and 17-year (1.256), 14-year and 18-year (2.094), 15-years and 16-year (0.456), 15-year and 17-year (1.037), 15-year and 18-year (1.875), 16-year and 17-year (1.494), 16-year and 18-year (2.331), and 17-year and 18-year (0.837) groups.

Table – 15 : Pairwise comparison among Group Means of MC_2 (Flexibility)

Group Means						Mean Difference	S. Error	t-value
13-Yrs.	14-Yrs.	15-Yrs.	16-Yrs.	17-Yrs.	18-Yrs			
15.47		15.91				0.438	0.208	2.11*
15.47			16.95			– 1.475	0.208	7.09*
15.47				17.78		– 2.312	0.208	11.12*
	15.69		16.95			–1.256	0.208	6.03*
	15.69			17.78		– 2.094	0.208	10.06*
		15.91	15.45			0.456	0.208	2.19*
		15.91		16.95		– 1.037	0.208	4.98*
		15.91			17.78	–1.875	0.208	9.01*
			15.45	16.95		– 1.494	0.208	7.18*
			15.45		17.78	–2.331	0.208	11.20*
				16.95	17.78	–0.837	0.208	4.02*

*Significant at 0.05 level, $t_{0.05}(78) = 1.97$

Table–16 describes the three-way ANOVA of MC_3. When source of variation was age, the calculated F-value of the six age groups (44.670) was higher than the tabulated value ($F_{0.05}5,936=2.22$). So, age is a contributing variable for difference in MC_3 among the six age groups of the study. When source of variation was gender the calculated F-value was 11.978 which was also significant at 0.05 level, ($F_{0.05}1,936=3.85$).

Table-16: Three-way ANOVA on MC_3 (ISP)

Source of Variations	df	SS	MSS	Calculated F-value	Tabulated F-Value
Age (A)	6 - 1 = 5	731.058	146.212	44.670*	$2.22 F_{0.05}$ (5,936)
Gender (G)	2 - 1 = 1	39.204	39.204	11.978*	$3.85 F_{0.05}$ (1,936)
Area (L)	2 - 1 = 1	28.704	28.704	8.770*	$3.85 F_{0.05}$ (1,936)
Interaction$_1$ (A × G)	(6-1) (2-1) = 5	262.783	52.567	16.057*	$2.22 F_{0.05}$ (5,936)
Interaction$_2$ (G × L)	(2-1) (2-1) = 1	39.204	39.204	11.978*	$3.85 F_{0.05}$ (1,936)
Interaction$_3$ (A × L)	(6-1) (2-1) = 5	130.833	26.167	7.994*	$2.22 F_{0.05}$ (5,936)
Interaction$_4$(A×G×L)	(6-1)(2-1)(2-1) = 5	11.958	2.392	0.731^{NS}	$2.22 F_{0.05}$ (5,936)
Error	N– (A×G×L) = 936	3063.650	3.273		
Total	960	204700.00			

*Significant at 0.05 level of significance

So, it is seen that boys and girls shows significant difference in MC_3. When the source of variation was area, the calculated F-value (8.770) was significant at 0.05 level of confidence and the calculated F-value was more than the tabulated F-value (3.85). So, in

MC_3, 'area' had an influence among the teenage students.

In Interaction$_1$ (Age × Gender) the calculated F-value (16.057) was more than the tabulated F-value (2.22) which denotes that when age and gender both are considered as the source of variation a significant difference is observed.

The calculated F-value in Interaction$_2$ (Gender × Area) which 11.978 was more than the tabulated F-value (3.85), that reveals that gender and area had a significant difference when both were considered as the source of variation.

In case of Interaction$_3$ (Age × Area) the calculated F-value (7.994) was more than the tabulated F-value (2.22) which denotes that there is a significant difference between age and area on MC_3.

When age, gender and area, all the three source of variations were considered all together in Interaction$_4$, the calculated F-value (0.731) was less than the tabulated F-value ($F_{0.05}5,936=2.22$), which reveals that there was no significant difference among the six age groups.

Table – 17 : Pairwise comparison among Group Means of MC_3 (ISP)

Group Means						Mean Difference	S. Error	t-value
13-Yrs.	14-Yrs.	15-Yrs.	16-Yrs.	17-Yrs.	18-Yrs			
13.62		14.38				0.763	0.202	3.77*
13.62				14.71		1.088	0.202	5.38*
13.62					16.21	2.594	0.202	12.84*
	13.77	14.38				0.612	0.202	3.02*
	13.77			14.71		0.938	0.202	4.65*
	13.77				16.21	2.444	0.202	12.09*
		14.38	13.96			0.419	0.202	2.07*
		14.38			16.21	1.831	0.202	9.06*
			13.96	14.71		0.744	0.202	3.68*
			13.96		16.21	2.250	0.202	11.13*
				14.71	16.21	1.506	0.202	7.45*

*Significant at 0.05 level, $t_{0.05}$ (78) = 1.97

Table-17 is representing the comparisons between two age group means which is found to be significantly different (P < 0.05) among the six age groups of MC_3. In pairwise comparisons, mean differences were significant between 13-year and 15-year (0.763), 13-year and 17-year (1.088), 13-year and 18-year (16.21), 14-year and 15-year (0.612), 14-year and 17-year (0.928), 14-year and 18-year (2.444), 15-year and 16-year (0.419),

15-year and 18-year (1831), 16-year and 17-year (0.744), 16-year and 18-year (2.250), 17-year and 18-year (1.506) groups.

Table – 18 : Three-way ANOVA on MC$_4$ (Fluency)

Source of Variations	df	SS	MSS	Calculated F-value	Tabulated F-Value
Age (A)	6 - 1 = 5	1317.85	263.571	79.233*	2.22F$_{0.05}$ (5,936)
Gender (G)	2 - 1 = 1	11.926	11.926	3.585^{NS}	3.85 F$_{0.05}$ (1,936)
Area (L)	2 - 1 = 1	10.626	10.626	3.194^{NS}	3.85 F$_{0.05}$ (1,936)
Interaction$_1$ (A × G)	(6-1)(2-1) = 5	277.080	55.416	16.659*	2.22F$_{0.05}$ (5,936)
Interaction$_2$ (G × L)	(2-1)(2-1) = 1	57.526	57.526	17.293*	3.85 F$_{0.05}$ (1,936)
Interaction$_3$ (A × L)	(6-1)(2-1) = 5	446.430	89.286	26.841*	2.22F$_{0.05}$ (5,936)
Interaction$_4$(A×G×L)	(6-1)(2-1)(2-1) = 5	37.055	7.411	2.228*	2.22F$_{0.05}$ (5,936)
Error	N - (A×G×L) = 936	3113.625	3.327		
Total	960	181883.000			

Significant at 0.05 level of significance

Table–18 depicts the three-way ANOVA of MC$_4$. When age was considered as the source of variation the calculated F-value of the six age groups was 79.233 which was significant 0.05 level of significance (F$_{0.05}$5,936=2.22). Therefore, a significant difference is observed when age is considered among the six age groups of the study in MC$_4$. When gender was considered as the source of variation the calculated F-value was 3.585 which was less than the tabulated F-value (3.85). So we can say that gender had no influence on MC$_4$ among the teenage students.

When age and gender were taken into consideration on Interaction$_1$ the calculated F-value (16.659) was more than the tabulated F-value (2.22) which indicates that there is a significant difference, where age and gender both were considered as the source of variation.

In Interaction$_2$ (gender × area) the calculated F-value (17.293) was more than the tabulated value (3.85) which indicates that there is a significant difference when gender and area together were considered as the source of variation.

When age and area were considered as the source of variation in Interaction$_3$ we observe that the calculated F-value (26.841) is more than the tabulated F-value (2.22) which reveals that on MC$_4$ there is a significant difference between age and area.

In case of Interaction$_4$ where age, gender and area, all the three sources of variation were combinedly considered the calculated F-value (2.228) was more than the tabulated F-value (F$_{0.05}$5,936=2.22), which depicts that there was a significant difference among the six age groups on MC$_4$ in this respect.

Table – 19 : Pairwise comparison among Group Means of MC_4 (Fluency)

Group Means						Mean Difference	S. Error	t-value
13-Yrs.	14-Yrs.	15-Yrs.	16-Yrs.	17-Yrs.	18-Yrs			
12.06	12.52					0.456	0.204	2.23*
12.06		13.73				1.663	0.204	8.15*
12.06			13.40			1.338	0.204	6.55*
12.06				13.90		1.838	0.204	9.00*
12.06					15.74	3.675	0.204	18.01*
	12.52	13.73				1.206	0.204	5.91*
	12.52		13.40			0.881	0.204	4.31*
	12.52			13.90		1.381	0.204	6.76*
	12.52				15.74	3.219	0.204	15.77*
		13.73			15.74	2.012	0.204	9.86*
			13.40	13.90		0.500	0.204	2.45*
			13.40		15.74	2.337	0.204	11.45*
				13.90	15.74	1.837	0.204	9.00*

*Significant at 0.05 level, $t_{0.05}(78) = 1.97$

Table-19 is representing the comparisons between two age group means which is found to be significantly different ($P < 0.05$) among the six age group means of MC_4. In pairwise comparisons on MC_4 mean differences were significant between 13-year and 14-year (0.456), 13-year and 15-year (1.663), 13-year and 16-year (1.338), 13-year and 17-year (1.838), 13-year and 18-year (3.675), 14-year and 15-year (1.206), 14-year and 16- year (0.881), 14-year and 17-year (1.381), 14-year and 18-year (3.219), 15-year and 18-year (2.012), 16-year and 17-year (0.500), 16-year and 18-year (2.337) and 17-year and 18-year (1.837) groups.

Table-20 reveals that the three-way ANOVA of MC_5. When age was considered as the source of variation the calculated F-value 56.667 was significant at 0.05 level of significance ($F_{0.05}5,936=2.22$). Hence, a significant difference among the six age groups is evident in MC_5 for age. When gender was the source of variation the calculated F-value =99.971 revealed a significant difference at 0.05 level ($F_{0.05}1,936=3.85$). So, a significant difference between boys and girls are found in MC_5. When the source of variation was area the calculated F-value (8.312) was more than tabulated F-value (3.85), therefore we can say that there is an influence of area on MC_5 among the teenage students.

Table – 20 : Three-way ANOVA on MC_5 (Elaboration)

Source of Variations	df	SS	MSS	Calculated F-value	Tabulated F-Value
Age (A)	6 - 1 = 5	2823.783	564.757	56.667*	$2.22 F_{0.05}$ (5,936)
Gender (G)	2 - 1 = 1	996.337	996.337	99.971*	$3.85 F_{0.05}$ (1,936)
Area (L)	2 - 1 = 1	82.838	82.838	8.312*	$3.85 F_{0.05}$ (1,936)
Interaction$_1$ (A × G)	(6-1) (2-1) = 5	1360.737	272.147	27.307*	$2.22 F_{0.05}$ (5,936)
Interaction$_2$ (G × L)	(2-1) (2-1) = 1	194.400	194.400	19.506*	$3.85 F_{0.05}$ (1,936)
Interaction$_3$ (A × L)	(6-1) (2-1) = 5	143.038	28.608	2.870*	$2.22 F_{0.05}$ (5,936)
Interaction$_4$(A×G×L)	(6-1)(2-1)(2-1) = 5	370.350	74.070	7.432*	$2.22 F_{0.05}$ (5,936)
Error	N -(A×G×L) = 936	9328.450	9.966		
Total	960	572492.000			

*Significant at 0.05 level of significance

In Interaction$_1$ (Age × Gender) the calculated F-value (27.307) was more than the tabulated F-value (3.85) which indicates that, there is a significant difference, when the source of variation, are age and gender together.

When we considered gender and area combinedly in Interaction$_2$ the calculated F-value (19.506) was more than the tabulated F-value (3.85) which signifies that there is a significant difference when we combinedly consider gender and area as the source of variation.

In case of Interaction$_3$, where age and area are the source of variation the calculated F-value (2.870) is more than the tabulated F-value (2.22) which indicates that there is a significant difference when age and area are considered on MC_5.

When age, gender and area all the three sources of variation were combinedly considered in Interaction$_4$ the calculated F-value (7.432) was more than the tabulated F-value ($F_{0.05}$5,936=2.22), which depicts that there were significant difference among the six age groups on MC_5 in this respect.

Table-21 represents the comparisons between two age group means found to be significantly different (P < 0.05) among the six age group means of MC_5. In pairwise group mean comparisons, mean differences were significant between 13-year and 14-year (0.962), 13-year and 15-year (3.525), 13-year and 16-year (5.300), 13-year and 17-year (2.169), 13-year and 18-year (2.056), 14-year and 15-year (2.563), 14-year and 16-year 94.337), 14-year and 17-year (1.206), 14-year and 18-yeas (1.094), 15-year and 16-year (1.775), 15-year and 17-year (1.356), 15-year and 18-year (1.469), 16-year and 17-year (3.31), 16- year and 18-year (3.244) and 17-year and 18-year (1.00) groups.

Table – 21 : Pairwise comparison among Group Means of MC_5 (Elaboration)

Group Means						Mean Difference	S. Error	t-value
13-Yrs.	14-Yrs.	15-Yrs.	16-Yrs.	17-Yrs.	18-Yrs			
21.75	22.71					0.962	0.353	2.72*
21.75		25.28				3.525	0.353	9.98*
21.75			27.05			5.300	0.353	15.01*
21.75				23.81		2.169	0.353	6.14*
21.75					24.81	2.056	0.353	5.82*
	22.71	25.28				2.563	0.353	7.26*
	22.71		27.05			4.337	0.353	12.28*
	22.71			23.81		1.206	0.353	3.41*
	22.71				24.81	1.094	0.353	2.83*
		25.28	27.05			1.775	0.353	5.03*
		25.28		23.81		1.356	0.353	3.84*
		25.28			24.81	1.469	0.353	4.16*
			27.05	23.81		3.131	0.353	8.86*
			27.05		24.81	3.244	0.353	9.18*
				23.81	24.81	1.000	0.353	2.83*

*Significant at 0.05 level, $t_{0.05}(78) = 1.97$

Table – 22 : Three-way ANOVA on MCT

Source of Variations	df	SS	MSS	Calculated F-value	Tabulated F-Value
Age (A)	6 - 1 = 5	14436.453	2887.309	56.109*	$2.22 F_{0.05}(5,936)$
Gender (G)	2 - 1 = 1	5553.626	5553.626	107.924*	$3.85 F_{0.05}(1,936)$
Area (L)	2 - 1 = 1	18.984	18.984	0.369^{NS}	$3.85 F_{0.05}(1,936)$
Interaction$_1$ (A × G)	(6-1)(2-1) = 5	820.768	164.154	3.190*	$2.22 F_{0.05}(5,936)$
Interaction$_2$ (G × L)	(2-1)(2-1) = 1	4631.968	926.394	18.003*	$3.85 F_{0.05}(1,936)$
Interaction$_3$ (A × L)	(6-1)(2-1) = 5	2448.159	489.632	9.515*	$2.22 F_{0.05}(5,936)$
Interaction$_4$ (A×G×L)	(6-1)(2-1)(2-1)= 5	914.551	914.551	17.773*	$2.22 F_{0.05}(5,936)$
Error	N-(A×G×L)= 936	48165.225	51.459		
Total	960	7480813.00			

*Significant at 0.05 level of significance

Table–22 describes the three-way ANOVA of MCT. When the source of variation was 'age', the calculated F-value (56.109) of the six age groups was significant at 0.05 level of significance. ($F_{0.05}5,936=2.22$). Hence, on MCT, significant difference was evident when age was considered as the variable. When gender was considered as the source of variation the calculated F-value (107.924) was more than the tabulated F-value ($F_{0.05}5,936=2.22$). So we observe a significant difference between boys and girls on MCT. When area was the source of variation the calculated F-value 0.369 was less than the tabulated F-value which shows that area had no significant difference in MCT among the teenage students.

When age and gender are combinedly considered in Interaction$_1$ we see that the calculated F-value (18.003) was more than the tabulated F-value (3.85) which signifies that there is a significant difference when age and gender together are the source of variation.

In Interaction$_2$ when gender and area were together considered as the source of variation the calculated F-value (17.773) was more than the tabulated F-value which reveals that there is a significant difference when on MC total.

When age and area are considered together as the source of variation in Interaction$_3$ the calculated F value (9.515) was more than the tabulated F-value (2.22) which shows that there is a significant difference when age and area are considered together on MC total.

In Interaction$_4$ (age × gender × area) when all the three sources of variations were considered combinedly the calculated F-value (3.190) was more than the tabulated F-value ($F_{0.05}5,936=2.22$) which reveals that there were significant difference among the six age group teenage students on MC total in this respect.

Table – 23: Pairwise comparison among Group Means of MCT

Group Means						Mean Difference	S. Error	t-value
13-Yrs.	14-Yrs.	15-Yrs.	16-Yrs.	17-Yrs.	18-Yrs			
81.90	83.91					2.019	0.802	2.51*
81.90		88.92				7.029	0.802	8.76*
81.90			88.85			6.950	0.802	8.66*
81.90				89.64		7.744	0.802	9.65*
81.90					93.68	11.781	0.802	14.68*
	83.91	88.92				5.006	0.802	6.24*
	83.91		88.85			4.931	0.802	6.14*
	83.91			89.64		5.725	0.802	7.13*
	83.91				93.68	9.762	0.802	12.17*
		88.92			93.68	4.756	0.802	5.93*
			88.85		93.68	4.831	0.802	6.02
				89.64	93.68	4.037	0.802	5.03*

*Significant at 0.05 level, $t_{0.05}(78) = 1.97$

Table-23 represents the pairwise comparison among group means which were found to be significantly different (P < 0.05) among the six age group means in MCT. The mean differences in pairwise comparisons were significant between 13-years and 14-years (2.019), 13-year and 15-year (7.029), 13-year and 16-year (6.950), 13-year and 17-year (7.744), 13-year and 18-year (11.781), 14-year and 15-year (5.006), 14-year and 16-year (4.931), 14-year and 17-year (5.725), 14-year and 18-year (9.762), 15-year and 18-year (4.756), 16-year and 18-year (4.831), 17-year and 18-year (4.037) groups.

Table – 24 : Pairwise comparison of Motor Creativity according to Gender

Variable	Group	Number	Mean	Mean Difference	SE_m	t-value
MC_1	Boys	480	20.171	1.323	0.130	10.77*
	Girls	480	18.848			
MC_2	Boys	480	16.844	1.263	0.131	9.64*
	Girls	480	15.581			
MC_3	Boys	480	14.650	0.404	0.129	3.13*
	Girls	480	14.246			
MC_4	Boys	480	13.452	0.223	0.138	1.62^{NS}
	Girls	480	13.675			
MC_5	Boys	480	25.110	2.038	0.269	7.58*
	Girls	480	23.073			
MCT	Boys	480	90.225	4.810	0.505	9.52*
	Girls	480	85.415			

*Significant at 0.05 level, $t_{0.05}$ (958) = 1.96

Table-24 represents the pair-wise comparisons of Motor Creativity according to gender. The mean difference in MC_1 between boys and girls groups was 1.323 with the t-value of 10.77 which was significant at 0.05 level of significance ($t_{0.05}$958=1.96). In case of MC_2 the mean difference between the boys and girls were 1.263 with t-value 9.64, which was significant at 0.05 level. In MC_3 the mean difference of boys and girls group were 0.404 with and the t-value of 3.13 was also significant at 0.05 level of significance. No significant difference was observed between the boys and the girls group according to the mean difference value of MC_4. In MC_5 the mean difference of the boys and girls group was 2.038 with the t-value 7.58, which was significant at 0.05 level. For Motor Creativity Total (MCT) the mean difference was 4.810 with the t-value 9.52 which was also significant at 0.05 level.

Table – 25 : Descriptive statistics of Motor Creativity for Early and Late Adolescent Groups

Group	Gender	Area	Number	MC$_1$ Mean (SD)	MC$_2$ Mean (SD)	MC$_3$ Mean (SD)	MC$_4$ Mean (SD)	MC$_5$ Mean (SD)	MCT Mean (SD)
Early Adolescent Group	Boys	Plane	120	19.91 (1.75)	16.55 (1.54)	14.42 (1.56)	12.95 (1.66)	23.99 (3.70)	87.80 (7.60)
		Hill	120	19.29 (1.88)	15.42 (1.84)	13.17 (1.80)	11.92 (1.85)	23.67 (3.80)	83.50 (8.05)
		Total	240	19.60 (1.84)	15.99 (1.79)	13.80 (1.79)	12.44 (1.83)	23.83 (3.74)	85.65 (8.10)
	Girls	Plane	120	19.17 (2.06)	15.48 (1.90)	14.21 (1.78)	13.30 (1.82)	22.43 (2.56)	84.70 (7.17)
		Hill	120	18.72 (2.40)	15.32 (2.62)	13.90 (2.52)	12.90 (2.52)	22.90 (3.98)	83.63 (10.39)
		Total	240	18.94 (2.24)	15.40 (2.29)	14.05 (2.18)	13.10 (2.20)	22.67 (3.35)	84.17 (8.93)
	Total	Plane	240	19.53 (1.94)	16.01 (1.81)	14.32 (1.67)	13.13 (1.75)	23.21 (3.27)	86.25 (7.53)
		Hill	240	19.00 (2.17)	15.37 (2.27)	13.53 (2.21)	12.41 (2.26)	23.30 (3.90)	83.57 (9.28)
		Total	480	19.27 (2.07)	15.70 (2.07)	13.92 (1.99)	12.77 (2.05)	23.25 (3.60)	84.91 (8.55)
Late Adolescent Group	Boys	Plane	120	20.77 (1.94)	18.00 (2.40)	15.62 (2.00)	14.22 (1.66)	26.54 (4.55)	94.87 (6.99)
		Hill	120	20.71 (1.99)	17.40 (2.17)	15.37 (2.41)	14.70 (3.11)	26.23 (3.80)	94.71 (8.14)
		Total	240	20.74 (1.96)	17.70 (2.30)	15.50 (2.21)	14.46 (2.50)	26.38 (4.18)	94.80 (7.57)
	Girls	Plane	120	18.66 (1.67)	15.98 (1.57)	14.21 (1.46)	13.34 (1.41)	22.22 (2.19)	84.45 (6.01)
		Hill	120	18.85 (2.33)	15.94 (1.88)	14.65 (2.16)	15.14 (2.46)	24.72 (4.36)	88.87 (7.53)
		Total	240	18.75 (2.02)	15.77 (1.73)	14.43 (1.86)	14.24 (2.19)	23.47 (3.66)	86.66 (7.15)
	Total	Plane	240	19.71 (2.09)	16.99 (2.26)	14.92 (1.88)	13.78 (1.60)	24.38 (4.17)	89.66 (8.34)
		Hill	240	19.78 (2.35)	16.47 (2.23)	15.01 (2.31)	14.92 (2.81)	25.48 (4.15)	91.79 (8.36)
		Total	480	19.74 (2.23)	16.73 (2.25)	14.97 (2.11)	14.35 (2.35)	24.93 (4.19)	90.72 (8.40)

SD = Standard Deviation.

Table–25 represents the descriptive statistics of Motor Creativity and its components of the early and the late adolescents groups. Each group of boys and girls in early and late adolescent group consisted of 240 subjects. In early adolescent plane boys (N = 120) the scores (mean ± SD) for MC_1 were 19.91 ± 1.75, for MC_2 16.55 ± 1.54, for MC_3 14.42 ± 1.56, for MC_4 12.95 ± 1.66, for MC_5 23.99 ± 3.70 and for MCT the score was 87.80 ± 7.60. Whereas, for early adolescent hill boys (N = 120) the scores were 19.29 ± 1.88 for MC_1, for MC_2 15.42 ± 1.84, for MC_3 13.17 ± 1.80, for MC_4 11.92 ± 1.85, for MC_5 23.67 ± 3.80 and for MCT the score was 83.50 ± 8.05. For total early adolescent boys (N = 240) the scores were 19.60 ± 1.84 for MC_1, 15.99 ± 1.79 for MC_2, 13.80 ± 1.79 for MC_3, 12.44 ± 1.83 for MC_4, 23.83 ± 3.74 for MC_5 and for MCT the score was 85.65 ± 8.10.

In early adolescent plane girls (N = 120), the scores were 19.17 ± 2.06 for MC_1, 15.48 ± 1.90 for MC_2, 14.21 ± 1.78 for MC_3, 13.30 ± 1.82 for MC_4, 22.43 ± 2.56 for MC_5 and for MCT the score was 84.70 ± 7.17. Whereas, for early adolescent hill girls (N = 120) the scores for MC_1 were 18.72 ± 2.40, for MC_2 15.32 ± 2.62, for MC_3 13.90 ± 2.52, for MC_4 12.90 ± 2.52, for MC_5 22.90 ± 3.98 and for MCT the score was 83.63 ± 19.39. For total early adolescent girls (N = 240), the scores were 18.94 ± 2.24 for MC_1, 15.40 ± 2.29 for MC_2, 14.05 ± 2.18 for MC_3, 13.10 ± 2.20 for MC_4, 22.67 ± 3.35 for MC_5 and 84.17 ± 8.93 for MCT.

For early adolescent plane boys and girls (N = 240), the score for MC_1 were 19.53 ± 1.94, for MC_2 16.01 ± 1.81, for MC_3 14.32 ± 1.67, for MC_4 13.13 ± 1.75, for MC_5 23.21 ± 3.27 and for MCT the score was 86.25 ± 7.53. Whereas for early adolescent hill boys and girls (N = 240) the score for MC_1 were 19.00 ± 2.17, 15.37 ± 2.27 for MC_2, 13.53 ± 2.21 for MC_3, 12.41 ± 2.26 for MC_4, 23.30 ± 3.90 for MC_5 and for MCT the score was 83.57 ± 9.28. For total early adolescent boys and girl (N = 480) the scores for MC_1 were 19.27 ± 2.07, for MC_2 15.70 ± 2.07, for MC_3 13.92 ± 1.99, for MC_4 12.77 ± 2.05, for MC_5 23.25 ± 3.60 and for MCT the score was 84.91 ± 8.55.

In late adolescent plane boys (N = 120) the scores (mean ± SD) for MC_1 were 20.77 ± 1.94, for MC_2 18.00 ± 2.40, for MC_3 15.62 ± 2.00, for MC_4 14.22 ± 1.66, for MC_5 26.54 ± 4.55 and for MCT the score was 94.87 ± 6.99. Whereas for late adolescent hill boys (N = 120), the scores were 20.71 ± 1.99 for MC_1, 17.40 ± 2.17 for MC_2, 15.37 ± 2.41 for MC_3, 14.70 ± 3.11 for MC_4, 26.23 ± 3.80 for MC_5 and 94.71 ± 8.14 for MCT. For the total late adolescent boys (plane + hill) where N = 240, the scores for MC_1 were 20.74 ± 1.96, for MC_2 17.70 ± 2.30, for MC_3 15.50 ± 2.21, for MC_4 14.46 ± 2.50, for MC_5 26.38 ± 4.18 and for MCT the score was 94.80 ± 7.57.

For late adolescent plane girls (N = 120) the scores were 18.66 ± 1.67 for MC_1, 15.98 ± 1.57 for MC_2, 14.21 ± 1.46 for MC_3, 13.34 ± 1.41 for MC_4, 22.22 ± 2.19 for MC_5 and 84.45 ± 6.01 for MCT. Whereas, for late adolescent hill girls (N = 120) the scores for MC_1 were 18.85 ± 2.33 for MC_2 were 15.94 ± 1.88, for MC_3 were 14.65 ± 2.16, for MC_4 were 15.14 ± 2.46, for MC_5 were 24.72 ± 4.36 and for MCT the score was 88.87 ± 7.53. When total girls of both hill and plane of the late adolescent group (N = 240) were taken together taken into consideration, the scores were 18.75 ± 2.02 for MC_1, 15.77 ± 1.73 for MC_2, 14.43 ± 1.86 for MC_3 14.24 ± 2.19 for MC_4, 23.47 ± 3.66 for MC_5 and 86.66 ± 7.15 for MCT.

For late adolescent plane boys and girls (N = 240), the score for MC_1 were 19.71 ± 2.09, for MC_2 16.99 ± 2.26, for MC_3 14.92 ± 1.88, for MC_4 13.78 ± 1.60, for MC_5 24.38 ± 4.17 and for MCT the score was 89.66 ± 8.34. For late adolescent hill boys and girls (N = 240), the MC_1 score were 19.78 ± 2.35, for MC_2 16.47 ± 2.23, for MC_3 15.01 ± 2.31, for MC_4 14.92 ± 2.81, for MC_5 25.48 ± 4.15 and for MCT it was 91.79 ± 8.36. For total late adolescent boys and girls (N = 480), the scores were 19.74 ± 2.23 for MC_1, 16.73 ± 2.25 for MC_2, 14.97 ± 2.11 for MC_3, 14.35 ± 2.35 for MC_4, 24.93 ± 4.19 for MC_5 and 90.72 ± 8.40 for total Motor Creativity.

Table – 26 : Three-way ANOVA on MC_1 (Originality) of Early and Late Adolescent Groups

Source of Variations	df	SS	MSS	Calculated F-value
Group (Gr.)	2 - 1 = 1	54.626	54.626	13.376*
Gender (G)	2 - 1 = 1	420.026	420.026	102.847*
Area (L)	2 - 1 = 1	12.834	12.834	3.143^{NS}
Interaction$_1$ (Gr. × G)	(2-1) (2-1) = 1	106.001	106.001	25.955*
Interaction$_2$ (Gr. × L)	(2-1) (2-1) = 1	21.901	21.901	5.363*
Interaction$_3$ (G × L)	(2-1) (2-1) = 1	2.501	2.501	0.612^{NS}
Interaction$_4$ (Gr. × G × L)	(2-1)(2-1)(2-1) = 1	0.084	0.084	0.021^{NS}
Error	952	3887.942	4.084	
Total	960	369897.00		

*Significant at 0.05 level of significance, $F_{0.05}$ (1, 952) = 3.85

Table–26 is representing the three-way ANOVA of MC_1 among the early and the late adolescent group. When group was considered as he source of variation the calculated F-value of the two groups (early and late adolescent) were 13.76 which was significant at 0.05 level of significance ($F_{0.05}$5,936=2.22). So, a significant difference in MC_1 was observed among the two groups (early and late adolescent) of the study. When gender was considered as the source of variation the calculated F-value (102.847) showed significant difference at 0.05 level. Hence both boys and girls showed significant difference in MC_1 when they are grouped as early and late adolescents. No significant difference was observed when area was considered as the source of variation in MC_1 as the calculated F-value (3.143) was less than the tabulated F-value (3.85). It signifies that area had no influence on MC_1 among the early and late adolescent group.

When group and gender both were considered as the source of variation in $Interaction_1$ the tabulated F-value ($F_{0.05}$ 1,936=3.85) was less than the calculated F-value (25.955) which reveals that there is a significant difference when group and gender were considered together as the source of variation in MC_1.

In case of $Interaction_2$ where group and area were considered combinedly the calculated F-value (5.363) was more than the tabulated F-value (3.85) which indicates that a significant difference is observed in MC_1 when group and area together were considered as the source of variation.

When gender and area together are considered as the source of variation in $Interaction_3$ the tabulated F-value (3.85) was more than the calculated F-value (0.612) which shows that no significant difference is observed when gender and area together were considered as the source of variation in MC_1.

In $Interaction_4$ (Group × Gender × Area) the calculated F-value (0.021) was less than the tabulated F-value ($F_{0.05}$5,936=2.22), which reveals that there was no significant difference among the two groups (early and late adolescent) in MC_1 when all the three source of variations (group, gender, area) together were taken into consideration.

Table – 27 : Pairwise comparison among the group means of MC_1 for early and late adolescent boys and girls

Group Means				Mean Difference	S. Error	t-value
EAB	EAG	LAB	LAG			
19.60	18.94			0.66	0.184	3.61*
19.60		20.74		1.14	0.184	6.33*
19.60			1875	0.85	0.184	4.66*
	18.94	20.74		1.80	0.184	9.78*
	18.94		18.75	1.13	0.184	6.14*
		20.74	18.75	1.99	0.184	10.81*

*Significant at 0.05 level, $t_{0.05}$ (78) = 1.97; NS = not significant

EAB=early adolescent boys, EAG=early adolescent girls, LAB=late adolescent boys, LAG=late adolescent girls

Table – 27 is representing the pairwise comparisons between two group means (i.e. the early adolescent and the late adolescent) which is found to be significantly different (P > 0.05) among the group means of MC_1. In pairwise comparison among the gender in the early adolescent group the mean difference (0.66) was significant. Between the boys of both the groups (early, late adolescent) the difference (1.14) was also significant. In between boys and girls of the late adolescent group difference observed was 1.99, and the difference of both the girls group (1.13) also significantly different.

The data of the table reveal that in pairwise comparison among the group means of MC_1 for early and late adolescent boys and girls, MC_1 values were all significant at 0.05 level. Hence, it is observed that all the pairwise group means were significantly different.

Table -28: Three-way ANOVA of MC_2 (Flexibility) of Early and Late Adolescent Group

Source of Variations	df	SS	MSS	Calculated F-value
Group (Gr.)	2 - 1 = 1	258.338	258.338	62.985*
Gender (G)	2 - 1 = 1	382.537	382.537	93.266*
Area (L)	2 - 1 = 1	80.504	80.504	19.628*
Interaction$_1$ (Gr. × G)	(2-1) (2-1) = 1	109.350	109.350	26.660*
Interaction$_2$ (Gr. × L)	(2-1) (2-1) = 1	1.067	1.067	0.260^{NS}
Interaction$_3$ (G × L)	(2-1) (2-1) = 1	18.150	18.150	4.425*
Interaction$_4$ (Gr.× G × L)	(2-1)(2-1)(2-1) = 1	10.004	10.004	2.439^{NS}
Error	952	3904.700	4.102	
Total	960	257096.00		

*Significant at 0.05 level of significance, $F_{0.05}$ (1, 952) = 3.85

Table-28 represents the three-way ANOVA of MC_2 among the early and the late adolescent group. When group was considered as the source of variation the F-value (62.985) of the early and late adolescent was significant at 0.05 level of significance ($F_{0.05}$ 1,936=3.85). So among the two groups of the study a significant difference was observed in MC_2. When gender was considered as the source of variation the calculated F-value (93.266) was more than the tabulated F-value (3.85) which reveals that both boys and girls of early and late adolescent group showed significant difference in MC_2. When area was considered as the source of variation the calculated F-value (19.628) was more than the tabulated F-value (3.85) which again indicates that area had a significant influence on MC_2 among the early and late adolescent groups.

In Interaction$_1$ where group and gender both were considered together as the source of variation the calculated F-value (26.660) was more than the tabulated F-value ($F_{0.05}$ 1,936=3.85), which shows that there is a significant difference when group and gender are considered together as the source of variation in MC_2.

When group and area were combinedly considered in Interaction$_2$ the calculated F-value (0.260) was less than the tabulated F-value (3.85) which indicates that group and area shows no significant difference among the early and late adolescents in MC_2.

In case of Interaction$_3$ when gender and area were combinedly considered the calculated F-value (4.425) was more than the tabulated F-value (3.85). So it can be said that gender and area when considered together as the source of variation, significant differences was observed among the early and the late adolescents.

When group, gender and area all three sources of variations were considered together in Interaction$_4$ the calculated F-value (2.439) was less than the tabulated F-value ($F_{0.05}$ 1,936=3.85), which reveals that no significant difference was observed among the early and the late adolescent groups in MC_2 in this respect.

Table – 29 : Pairwise comparison among the group means of MC_2 for early and late adolescent boys and girls

Group Means				Mean Difference	S. Error	t-value
EAB	EAG	LAB	LAG			
15.28	15.40			0.58	0.43	1.19 [NS]
15.28		18.26		2.27	0.43	5.27*
15.28			15.76	0.22	0.43	0.51 [NS]
	15.40	18.26		2.66	0.43	6.18*
	15.40		15.76	0.36	0.43	0.83 [NS]
		18.26	15.76	2.50	0.43	5.81*

*Significant at 0.05 level, $t_{0.05}$ (78) = 1.97; NS = not significant
EAB=early adolescent boys, EAG=early adolescent girls, LAB=late adolescent boys, LAG=late adolescent girls

Table-29 is representing the pairwise comparisons between two group means (i.e., EA, LA) in MC_2 which is found to be significant at 0.05 level, except in two cases. When gender was taken into consideration, the pairwise comparison between the early adolescent boys and girls (EAB – EAG = 0.58) showed no significant differences. But when early and late adolescent boys were compared they showed significant difference (2.27). Early adolescent girls showed no significant difference when compared with late adolescent girls (0.36). In between boys and girls in the late adolescent group, significant difference (2.50) was observed in MC_2.

From the above table it appears that in pairwise comparison among the group means of MC_2 early adolescent boys when compared with early adolescent girls and when EAG were compared with LAG they showed no significant difference.

Table – 30 : Three-way ANOVA of MC_3 (ISP) of Early and Late Adolescent Group

Source of Variations	df	SS	MSS	Calculated F-value
Group (Gr.)	2 - 1 = 1	258.338	258.338	64.896*
Gender (G)	2 - 1 = 1	39.204	39.204	9.848*
Area (L)	2 - 1 = 1	28.704	28.704	7.211*
Interaction$_1$ (Gr. × G)	(2-1) (2-1) = 1	105.337	105.337	26.461*
Interaction$_2$ (Gr. × L)	(2-1) (2-1) = 1	45.938	45.938	11.540*
Interaction$_3$ (G × L)	(2-1) (2-1) = 1	39.204	39.204	9.848*
Interaction$_4$ (Gr.× G × L)	(2-1)(2-1)(2-1)= 1	0.938	0.938	0.236^{NS}
Error	952	3789.733	3.981	
Total	960	204700.00		

Significant at 0.05 level of significance, $F_{0.05}$ (1, 952) = 3.85

Table-30 represents the three-way ANOVA of MC_3 among the early and the late adolescent group. When group was considered as the source of variation the tabulated F-value ($F_{0.05}$ 1,936=3.85) was less than the calculated F-value which indicates that there is a significant difference among the two age groups (late and early adolescent) in MC_3. When gender was considered as the source of variation the calculated F-value (9.848) was more than the tabulated F-value (3.85). So we can say that both boys and girls of early and late adolescent groups had a significant difference in MC_3. Significant difference was observed when area was considered as a source of variation the calculated F-value (7.211) was more than the tabulated F-value (3.85) which reveals that area had an influence on MC_3 among the early and late adolescent groups.

When group and gender both were together considered in Interaction$_1$ the calculated F-value (26.461) was more than the tabulated F-value (3.85). It signifies that there is a significant difference when group and gender were considered together as the source of variation.

In Interaction$_2$ (group × area) the calculated F-value (11.546) was more than the tabulated F value ($F_{0.05}$5,936=2.22), which showed significant difference when group and area together were considered as the source of variation in MC_3.

In case of Interaction$_3$ when gender and area were together considered the calculated F value (9.848) was more than the tabulated F-value (3.85) which reveals that there is a significant difference of gender and age on MC_3.

In Interaction$_4$ (group × gender × area) the calculated F-value (0.236) was less than the tabulated F value (3.85) which shows that when group, gender and area were considered together as the source of variation no significant difference was found among the two groups (early and late adolescent) in MC_3.

Table – 31: Pairwise comparison among the group means of MC_3 of Early and Late Adolescent Groups

Group Means				Mean Difference	S. Error	t-value
EAB	EAG	LAB	LAG			
13.80	14.05			1.16	0.18	6.44*
13.80		15.50		2.55	0.18	14.16*
13.80			14.43	0.36	0.18	2.00*
	14.05	15.50		3.71	0.18	20.61*
		15.50	14.43	1.06	0.18	5.88*
	14.05		14.43	0.80	0.18	4.44*

*Significant at 0.05 level, $t_{0.05}$ (78) = 1.97; NS = not significant

EAB=early adolescent boys, EAG=early adolescent girls, LAB=late adolescent boys, LAG=late adolescent girls

Table-31 reveals that the pairwise comparisons between two group means i.e., the EAB and LAG groups in MC_3 which is found to be significant at 0.05 level. In between gender and in between groups when compared they showed significant differences. Comparison between the genders of early and late adolescent groups yielded significant differences in MC_3.

Table – 32 : Three-way ANOVA of MC_4 (Fluency) of Early and Late Adolescent Groups

Source of Variations	df	SS	MSS	Calculated F-value
Group (Gr.)	2 - 1 = 1	596.926	596.926	131.108*
Gender (G)	2 - 1 = 1	11.926	11.926	2.619^{NS}
Area (L)	2 - 1 = 1	10.626	10.626	2.334^{NS}
Interaction$_1$ (Gr. × G)	(2-1)(2-1) = 1	47.259	47.259	10.380*
Interaction$_2$ (Gr. × L)	(2-1)(2-1) = 1	206.276	206.276	45.306*
Interaction$_3$ (G × L)	(2-1)(2-1) = 1	57.526	57.526	12.635*
Interaction$_4$ (Gr. × G × L)	(2-1)(2-1)(2-1) = 1	7.176	7.176	1.576^{NS}
Error	952	4334.408	4.553	
Total	960	181883.00		

*Significant at 0.05 level of significance, $F_{0.05}$ (1, 952) = 3.85

The table represents that in pairwise comparison between EAB and EAG, LAB and LAG, EAG and LAG, EAB and LAB, all showed significant difference.

Table–32 represents the three-way ANOVA of MC_4 among the early and late adolescent groups. When group was considered as the source of variation the calculated F-value (131.08) was more than the tabulated F-value ($F_{0.05}$ 1,936=3.85). So, a significant difference in MC_4 was observed among the two groups (early and late adolescent) of the study. When gender was considered as the source of variation the calculated F-value (2.619) was less than the tabulated F-value (3.85) which reveals that gender had no influence on MC_4. No significant difference was found when area was considered as the source of variation in MC_4. Here the calculated F-value (2.334) had no significant influence on MC_4 among the early and the late adolescent groups.

In Interaction$_1$ where group and gender together were considered as the source of variation the calculated F-value (10.380) was significant at 0.05 level. Hence, it reveals that group and gender when considered together showed significant difference in MC_4.

When group and area were considered combinedly in Interaction$_2$ the calculated F-value (45.306) was more than the tabulated F-value ($F_{0.05}$5,936=2.22), which reveals that group and area had an influence on MC_4.

In Interaction$_3$ where gender and area are together considered as the source of variation the calculated F-value (12.635) was significant at 0.05 level of confidence. Hence gender and area had an influence on MC_4 among the early and the late adolescent groups.

In case of Interaction$_4$ where group, gender and area were together taken into consideration as the source of variation no significant difference at 0.05 level was observed. The calculated F-value (1.576) was less than the tabulated F-value (3.85) which reveals that there was no significant difference in MC_4 when all the three sources of variation (group, gender, area) were taken together into consideration.

Table-33 is representing the pairwise comparisons between two group means which is found to be significantly different ($P < 0.05$) among the group means of MC_4. In pairwise comparison among the gender in early adolescent group, mean differences were significant (3.47). When boys of two groups (EAB and LAB) were compared, they also showed significant difference (2.02). Early adolescent girls when compared with late adolescent girls they showed significant difference (1.35) but boys and girls of the same age group did not show any significant difference (0.22).

Table – 33 : Pairwise comparison among the group means of MC_4 of Early and Late Adolescent Groups

Group Means				Mean Difference	S. Error	t-value
EAB	EAG	LAB	LAG			
12.44	13.10			0.66	0.19	3.47*
12.44		14.46		2.02	0.19	10.63*
12.44			14.24	1.80	0.19	9.47*
	13.10	14.46		1.35	0.19	7.10*
	13.10		14.24	1.13	0.19	5.94*
		14.46	14.24	0.22	0.19	1.15 NS

*Significant at 0.05 level, $t_{0.05}$ (78) = 1.97; NS = not significant

EAB=early adolescent boys, EAG=early adolescent girls, LAB=late adolescent boys, LAG=late adolescent girls

This table reveals that the boys when compared with girls of the late adolescent group they showed no significant difference but the other group, i.e., in early adolescence both the genders showed significant difference in MC_4.

Table – 34 : Three-way ANOVA of MC_5 (Elaboration) of Early and Late Adolescent Groups

Source of Variations	df	SS	MSS	Calculated F-value
Group (Gr.)	2 - 1 = 1	676.704	676.704	49.393*
Gender (G)	2 - 1 = 1	996.337	996.337	72.723
Area (L)	2 - 1 = 1	82.837	82.837	6.046*
Interaction$_1$ (Gr. × G)	(2-1)(2-1) = 1	183.750	183.750	13.412*
Interaction$_2$ (Gr. × L)	(2-1)(2-1) = 1	62.017	62.017	4.527*
Interaction$_3$ (G × L)	(2-1)(2-1) = 1	194.406	194.400	14.189*
Interaction$_4$ (Gr. × G × L)	(2-1)(2-1)(2-1) = 1	61.004	61.004	4.453*
Error	952	13042.883	13.701	
Total	960	572492.00		

*Significant at 0.05 level of significance, $F_{0.05}$ (1, 952) = 3.85

Table–34 represents the three-way ANOVA of MC_5 of early and late adolescent groups. When group was considered as the source of variation the calculated F-value of the two groups (early and late adolescent) was 49.393 which was significant at 0.05 level of significance ($F_{0.05}$5,936=2.22). So a significant difference was observed in the early and the late adolescent groups on MC_5. When gender was taken into consideration the calculated F-value (72.723) showed significant difference at 0.05 level. Hence both boys and girls of the early and late adolescent groups showed significant difference in MC_5. Significant difference was observed when area was considered as the source of variation in MC_5 as the calculated F-value (6.046) was more than the tabulated F-value (3.85).

In Interaction$_1$ where group and gender were together taken into consideration the calculated F-value (13.412) was significant at 0.05 level, which indicates that group and gender when taken together had an influence on MC_5 among the early and the late adolescent groups.

In case of Interaction$_2$ where group and area were combinedly taken into consideration the calculated F-value (4.527) was more than the tabulated F-value (3.85) which indicates that a significant difference is observed in MC_5 among the two age groups (early and late adolescent).

In case of Interaction$_3$ where gender and area were taken into consideration as the source of variation the calculated F-value (14.189) showed a significant difference at 0.05 level of significance ($F_{0.05}5,936=2.22$). This indicates that there was a significant difference in MC_5 when gender and area were together considered.

In Interaction$_4$ (group × gender × area) the calculated F-value (4.453) was more than the tabulated F value (3.85) which signifies that there was a significant difference among the early and the late adolescent groups in MC_4 when all the three sources of variation (group, gender, area) were taken into consideration.

Table – 35 : Pairwise comparison among the group means of MC_5 for early and late adolescent boys and girls

Group Means				Mean Difference	S. Error	t-value
EAB	EAG	LAB	LAG			
23.83	22.67			1.16	0.33	3.51*
23.83		26.38		2.55	0.33	7.72*
23.83			23.47	0.35	0.33	1.06 NS
	22.67	26.38		3.71	0.33	11.24*
	22.67		23.47	0.80	0.33	2.42*
		26.38	23.47	2.91	0.33	8.81*

Significant at 0.05 level, $t_{0.05}$ (78) = 1.97; NS = not significant

EAB=early adolescent boys, EAG=early adolescent girls, LAB=late adolescent boys, LAG=late adolescent girls

Table-35 is representing the pairwise comparison between two group means (EA, LA) which is significantly different ($P < 0.05$) among the group means of MC_5. In between gender of the early adolescent group significant differences were observed (1.16). When the boys of the two groups were compared significant difference (2.55) was found. Between the LAB and LAG also significant difference occurred (8.81). When early adolescent girls were compared with late adolescent girls in MC_5 they also showed significant difference (2.42). Only when the early adolescent boys were compared with the late adolescent girls they showed no significant difference (0.35).

Table – 36 : Three-way ANOVA of MCT of Early and Late Adolescent Groups

Source of Variations	df	SS	MSS	Calculated F-value
Group (Gr.)	2 - 1 = 1	8102.626	8102.626	132.236*
Gender (G)	2 - 1 = 1	5553.626	5553.626	90.636*
Area (L)	2 - 1 = 1	18.984	18.984	0.310^{NS}
Interaction$_1$ (Gr. × G)	(2-1)(2-1) = 1	2650.026	2650.026	43.249*
Interaction$_2$ (Gr. × L)	(2-1)(2-1) = 1	1389.609	1389.609	22.679*
Interaction$_3$ (G × L)	(2-1)(2-1) = 1	914.551	914.551	14.926*
Interaction$_4$ (Gr. × G × L)	(2-1)(2-1)(2-1) = 1	27.676	27.676	0.452^{NS}
Error	952	58332.725	61.274	
Total	960	7480813.000		

*Significant at 0.05 level of significance, $F_{0.05}$ (1, 952) = 3.85

Table–36 represents the three-way ANOVA of MCT of early and late adolescent groups. When group was considered as the source of variation the calculated F-value of the early and the late adolescent groups (132.236) was significant at 0.05 level ($F_{0.05}$5,936=2.22). So, in MCT a significant difference was observed in the early and the late adolescent groups. When gender was taken into consideration the calculated F-value (90.636) showed significant difference. Hence, a difference was observed on MC total in the early and late adolescent groups. But area did not show any significant difference in MCT.

In Interaction$_1$ where group and gender were taken together into consideration the calculated F-value (43.249) was more than the tabulated F-value ($F_{0.05}$ 1,936=3.85), which reveals that when group and gender are considered together a significant difference is observed on MCT.

When group and area combinedly were taken into consideration as the source of variation in Interaction$_2$ the calculated F-value (22.679) were more than the tabulated F-value (3.85) which indicates that a significant difference is observed in MCT when group (early and late adolescent) and area are considered together.

In Interaction$_3$ (Gender × Area) the calculated F-value (14.926) was more than the tabulated F-value ($F_{0.05}$5,936=2.22), which indicates a significant difference when gender and area were combinedly taken into consideration on MCT.

When age, gender and area all the three sources of variation were taken together into consideration in Interaction$_4$ the calculated F-value (0.452) was less than the tabulated F-value (3.85) which indicates that there were no significant difference among the early and the late adolescent groups on MCT in this respect.

Table – 37 : Pairwise comparison among the group means of MCT for early and late adolescent boys and girls

Group Means				Mean Difference	S. Error	t-value
EAB	EAG	LAB	LAG			
23.83	22.67			1.16	0.33	3.51*
23.83		26.38		2.55	0.33	7.72*
23.83			23.47	0.35	0.33	1.06^{NS}
	22.67	26.38		3.71	0.33	1.24*
	22.67		23.47	0.80	0.33	2.42*
		26.38	23.47	2.91	0.33	8.81*

*Significant at 0.05 level, $t_{0.05}$ (78) = 1.97; NS = not significant
EAB=early adolescent boys, EAG=early adolescent girls, LAB=late adolescent boys, LAG=late adolescent girls

Table–37 is representing the pairwise comparison between two group means (EA, LA) which is significantly different ($P < 0.05$) among the group means of MC$_5$. In between gender of the early adolescent group significant difference (1.16) was observed. When the two boys groups were compared, significant difference (2.55) was found. Between the LAB and LAG also significant difference (2.91) occurred. When early adolescent girls were compared with late adolescent girls in MC$_5$ they also showed significant difference (0.80). Only when the early adolescent boys were compared with the adolescent girls they showed no significant difference (0.35).

Table–38 represents the ANOVA results of Motor Creativity according of six age groups. When age was considered as the source of variation the calculated as the source of variation the calculated F value for MC$_1$ was 12.83, for MC$_2$ – 41.79, for MC$_3$ – 44.67, for MC$_4$ – 79.23, for MC$_5$ – 56.66, for MCT - 56.10. All the calculated F-values was more than the tabulated F-value ($F_{0.05}$5,936=2.22), which indicates that age had a significant difference among six age groups.

Table – 38 : ANOVA results of Motor Creativity according to Six Age Groups

Source of variation	df	MC_1	MC_2	MC_3	MC_4	MC_5	MCT	Tabulated F-value
Age (A)	5	12.83*	41.79*	44.67*	79.23*	56.66*	56.10*	$2.22 F_{0.05}(5,936)$
Gender (G)	1	110.38*	111.04*	11.97*	3.58*	99.97*	107.92*	$3.85 F_{0.05}(1,936)$
Area (L)	1	3.371*	23.36*	8.77*	3.19*	8.31*	0.369^{NS}	$3.85 F_{0.05}(1,936)$
Interaction$_1$ (A × G)	5	6.93*	13.84*	16.06*	16.66*	27.36*	3.19*	$2.22 F_{0.05}(5,936)$
Interaction$_2$ (G × A)	1	0.657^{NS}	5.269*	11.98*	17.29*	19.50*	18.00*	$3.85 F_{0.05}(1,936)$
Interaction$_3$ (A × L)	5	5.775*	3.117*	7.99*	26.84*	2.87*	9.51*	$2.22 F_{0.05}(5,936)$
Interaction$_4$ (A×G×L)	5	1.073^{NS}	2.718*	0.731^{NS}	2.228*	7.43*	17.77*	$2.22 F_{0.05}(5,936)$

*Significant at 0.05 level, NS = Not Significant

When gender was considered as the source of variation, the calculated F-value for MC_1 was 110.38, for MC_2 - 111.04, for MC_3 - 11.97, for MC_4 - 3.58, for MC_5 - 99.97 and for MC Total - 107.92 which were all significant at 0.05 level. When area was considered as the source of variation, the calculated F-value for MC_1 - 3.37, MC_2 - 23.36, MC_3 - 8.77, MC_4 - 3.19, MC_5 - 8.31 were significant at 0.05 level, except the calculated value of MCT (0.369) was not significant at 0.05 level. In Interaction$_1$ when age and gender were taken into consideration together, all the calculated values of MC_1 - 6.93, MC_2 - 13.84, MC_3 - 16.06, MC_4 - 16.66, MC_5 - 27.30 and MCT - 3.19 were more than the tabulated F-value. So significant difference existed when age and gender were considered together. When gender and area are considered together in Interaction$_2$, the calculated F-values for MC_2 - 5.269, MC_3 - 11.98, MC_4 - 17.29, MC_5 - 19.50 and MCT - 18.00 were significant at 0.05 level, except the calculated F-value of MC_1 - 0.657 was not significant at 0.05 level. In case of Interaction$_3$ when age and area were considered together the calculated F-value for MC_1 - 5.775, MC_2 - 3.117, MC_3 - 7.99, MC_4 - 26.84, MC_5 - 2.87 and MCT - 9.51 were greater than the tabulated F-value ($F_{0.05}5,936=2.22$), which indicates that all the motor creativity components were significant at 0.05 level of significance in this regard. When age, gender and area were together taken into consideration (Interaction$_4$), the calculated F-value for MC_2 - 2.718, MC_4 - 2.228, MC_5 - 7.43 and MCT - 17.77 were significant at 0.05 level, whereas the calculated F-value of MC_1 - 1.073 and MC_3 - 0.731 were less than the tabulated F-value (2.22).

Table – 39 : ANOVA results of Motor Creativity of Early and Late Adolescent Groups

Source of variation	df	MC_1	MC_2	MC_3	MC_4	MC_5	MCT	Tabulated F-value
Group	1	13.37*	62.98*	64.89*	131.11*	49.39*	132.23*	2.22 $F_{0.05}$ (1, 936)
Gender	1	102.84*	93.26*	9.85*	2.62*	72.72*	90.63*	2.22 $F_{0.05}$ (1, 936)
Area	1	3.14*	19.62*	7.21*	2.33*	6.04*	0.310^{NS}	2.22 $F_{0.05}$ (1, 936)
Interaction$_1$ (Age × Gender)	1	25.95*	26.66*	26.46*	10.38*	13.41*	43.25*	2.22 $F_{0.05}$ (1, 936)
Interaction$_2$ (Gender × Area)	1	5.36*	0.260^{NS}	11.54*	45.30*	4.53*	22.68*	2.22 $F_{0.05}$ (1, 936)
Interaction$_3$ (Age × Area)	1	0.612^{NS}	4.42*	9.85*	12.63*	14.18*	14.93*	2.22 $F_{0.05}$ (1, 936)
Interaction$_4$ (Age × Gender × Area)	1	0.021^{NS}	2.44*	0.236^{NS}	1.57^{NS}	4.45*	0.452^{NS}	2.22 $F_{0.05}$ (1, 936)

Significant at 0.05 level, NS = Not Significant

Table-39 represents the ANOVA results of Motor Creativity of early and late adolescent groups. When group was considered as the source of variation the calculated F-value for MC_1 was 13.37, for MC_2 - 62.98, for MC_3 - 64.89, for MC_4 - 131.11, for MC_5 - 49.39 and for MCT was 132.63. All calculated F-values ($F_{0.05}$5,936=2.22) were significant at 0.05 level. When gender was considered as the source of variation the calculated F-value for MC_1 was 102.84, for MC_2 - 93.26, MC_3 - 9.85, for MC_4 - 2.62, MC_5 - 72.72, MCT - 90.63. All the calculated F-values were more than the tabulated F-value (2.22) which indicates that the motor creativity components were significant when gender was considered. When area was considered as the source of variation the calculated F-value for MC_1 - 3.14, MC_2 - 19.62, MC_3 - 7.21, MC_4 - 2.33, MC_5 - 6.04 were significant at 0.05 level, where MC Total (0.310) did not show significant difference at 0.05 level.

When age and gender were together considered in Interaction$_1$ the calculated F-value for MC_1 was 25.95, for MC_2 - 26.66, for MC_3 - 26.46, for MC_4 - 10.38, for MC_5 - 13.41 and for MCT - 43.25. All the calculated values were significant at 0.05 level.

When gender and area were considered together the calculated F-value for MC_1 was 5.36, for MC_3 - 11.54, for MC_4 - 45.30, for MC_5 - 4.53, for MCT - 22.68, and the values were all significant at 0.05 level, except the calculated value of MC_2 (0.260), which was not significant at 0.05 level. When age and area were considered together (Interaction$_3$) the calculated F-value for MC_2 - 4.42, for MC_3 - 9.85, for MC_4 - 12.63, for MC_5 - 14.18 and for

MCT -14.93 were significant at 0.05 level. The calculated F-value for MC_1 (0.612) was less than the required value to be significant at 0.05 level.

When age, gender and area were taken together, the calculated F-value for MC_2 - 2.44 and MC_5 - 4.45 were significant whereas the calculated F-value for MC_1 - 0.021, for MC_3 - 0.236, for MC_4 - 1.57 and for MCT - 0.452 were not significant.

Table – 40 : Correlation Matrix on Motor Creativity and other three variables of Early Adolescent Boys and Girls

	MC_1	MC_2	MC_3	MC_4	MC_5	MC Total	AA	I	AM
MC_1	1	**0.774***	**0.618***	**0.497***	**0.293***	**0.783***	**0.375***	**0.347***	**0.375***
		0.654*	0.597*	0.488*	0.272*	0.805*	0.571*	0.548*	0.486*
MC_2		1	**0.742***	**0.587***	**0.248***	**0.810***	**0.331***	**0.338***	**0.305***
			0.582*	0.418*	0.113	0.729*	0.477*	0.474*	0.433*
MC_3			1	**0.731***	**0.151***	**0.762***	**0.311***	**0.324***	**0.241***
				0.602*	0.179*	0.738*	0.496*	0.524*	0.397*
MC_4				1	**0.213***	**0.728***	**0.295***	**0.422***	**0.261***
					0.184*	0.707*	0.500*	0.645*	0.370*
MC_5					1	**0.667***	**0.350***	**0.593***	**0.327***
						0.582*	0.391*	0.415*	0.306*
MCT						1	**0.458***	**0.597***	**0.420***
							0.682*	0.729*	0.544*
AA							1	**0.625***	**0.590***
								0.698*	0.514*
I								1	**0.528***
									0.540*
AM									1

AA = Academic Achievement; I = Intelligence; AM = Achievement Motivation
*Correlation is significant at 0.05 level, r values for male group are in bold font

Table-40 represents the correlation matrix among motor creativity and its five components with academic achievement, intelligence and achievement motivation variables in early adolescent boys and girls group. The correlation values of boys group have been presented in "bold font". In case of early adolescent boys group the correlations among the variables were significant at 0.05 level in all the cases. On the contrary in girls group, all the correlation values were significant at 0.05 level except the relationship between MC_5 to MC_2 with the correlation value 0.113 which was less than the tabulated 'r' value required to be significant at 0.05 level of significance.

The relationship between motor creativity total (MCT) and the other three variables, i.e. academic achievement (AA), intelligence and achievement motivation (AM) of early adolescent boys and girls were significantly correlated. For MCT to AA it was 0.458 for male and 0.682 for female students; for MCT to intelligence it was 0.597 for male and 0.729 for female; for MCT to AM it was 0.420 for male and 0.544 for female. The relationship between AA and intelligence was significant for both groups (male $r = 0.625$, female $r = 0.698$) and for AA and AM it was 0.590 for male and 0.514 for female students. In case of intelligence and AM the relationships were also significant (male $r = 0.582$, female $r = 0.540$).

Table – 41 : Correlation Matrix on Motor Creativity and other three variables of Late Adolescent Boys and Girls

	MC_1	MC_2	MC_3	MC_4	MC_5	MC Total	AA	I	AM
MC_1	1	**0.875***	**0.507***	**0.482***	**0.082**	**0.713***	**0.061**	**0.179***	**0.180***
		0.842*	0.548*	0.318*	0.078	0.687*	0.409*	0.545*	0.315*
MC_2		1	**0.681***	**0.568***	**0.244***	**0.643***	**0.027**	**0.008**	**0.141***
			0.507*	0.248*	0.001	0.839*	0.439*	0.580*	0.307*
MC_3			1	**0.732***	**– 0.188***	**0.711***	**0.061**	**0.007**	**0.128**
				0.513*	0.004	0.678*	0.334*	0.410*	0.210*
MC_4				1	**0.206***	**0.674***	**0.167***	**0.035**	**0.056**
					0.049	0.607*	0.210*	0.345*	0.141*
MC_5					1	**0.331***	**0.213***	**0.342***	**0.163***
						0.549*	0.168*	0.206*	0.256*
MCT						1	**0.066**	**0.243***	**0.241***
							0.447*	0.612*	0.392*
AA							1	**0.481***	**0.318***
								0.525*	0.506*
I								1	**0.576***
									0.410*
AM									1

AA = Academic Achievement; I = Intelligence; AM = Achievement Motivation
*Correlation is significant at 0.05 level, r values for male group are in bold font

Table–41 represents the correlation matrix among motor creativity and its five components in late adolescent boys and girls group. In boys group, the relationship among the Motor Creativity and its components were found to be significant in all the cases except the relationships between MC_1 and MC_5 ($r = 0.082$) was not statistically significant. The relationship between academic achievement and the remaining variables were found to be significant in two cases that were for MC_4 and MC_5 and MCT along with the remaining motor creativity components i.e. MC_1, MC_2, and MC_3 the relationship were not significant.

The relationship between intelligence with other variables were significant in four cases namely with MC_1, MC_5, MCT and academic achievement. The remaining three cases i.e. MC_2, MC_3, MC_4 the relationships were not significant. There were significant relationships between achievement motivation and MCT and the three motor creativity components i.e., MC_1, MC_2 and MC_5. The relationship between motivation and MC_3 and MC_4 were not significant. Significant relationship were observed between motivation and academic achievement, motivation and intelligence in the group. In the late adolescent girls group consistent result were observed with one exception on the relationships among the motor creativity and its components with the other three variables. The exceptional result was that there were no significant relationship between MC_5 with other four motor creativity components ($MC_1 - MC_4$). Whereas in all the remaining cases the correlations were found to be significant.

Table – 42 : Correlation Matrix on Motor Creativity and other three variables of Boys and Girls group

	MC_1	MC_2	MC_3	MC_4	MC_5	MC Total	AA	I	AM
MC_1	1	0.741*	0.800*	0.532*	0.251*	0.782*	0.201*	0.382*	0.314*
		0.640*	0.568*	0.387*	0.167*	0.738*	0.498*	0.378*	0.401*
MC_2		1	0.749*	0.643*	0.080	0.759*	0.148*	0.314*	0.288*
			0.543*	0.352*	0.071	0.697*	0.443*	0.418*	0.373*
MC_3			1	0.775*	0.080	0.775*	0.094*	0.315*	0.237*
				0.563*	0.100*	0.716*	0.407*	0.387*	0.307*
MC_4				1	0.084*	0.749*	0.022	0.347*	0.209*
					0.137*	0.668*	0.316*	0.404*	0.248*
MC_5					1	0.560*	0.266*	0.539*	0.285*
						0.557*	0.259*	0.228*	0.279*
MCT						1	0.229*	0.580*	0.382*
							0.550*	0.515*	0.487*
AA							1	0.492*	0.439*
								0.459*	0.505*
I								1	0.561*
									0.379*
AM									1

AA = Academic Achievement; I = Intelligence; AM = Achievement Motivation
*Correlation is significant at 0.05 level, r values for male group are in bold font

Table–42 represents the correlation matrix on motor creativity and the other three variables of total boys (N = 480) and girls (N = 480) group. In boys group the correlation between motor creativity variables were found to be significant in all the cases except the two relationships those were between MC_5 to MC_2 and MC_5 to MC_3. The correlation value of MC_4 and academic achievement was less than the tabulated r-value and the remaining correlation values were found to be significant at 0.05 level of significance. The relationships between intelligence and other variables were found to be significant as per 'r' value. Achievement motivation and other variables were also found to be significant. In case of girls the relationships between motor creativity and its components with the other variables were found significant in all cases with one exception that was, the relationship between MC_2 and MC_5 which was not significant as per the calculated 'r' value = 0.071.

Table – 43 : Correlation Matrix on Motor Creativity and other three variables of the total group

	MC_1	MC_2	MC_3	MC_4	MC_5	MC Total	AA	I	AM
MC_1	1	0.349*	0.556*	0.395*	0.262*	0.736*	0.343*	0.362*	0.465*
MC_2		1	0.336*	0.274*	0.073*	0.390*	0.100*	0.137*	0.227*
MC_3			1	0.667*	0.110*	0.743*	0.245*	0.279*	0.405*
MC_4				1	0.097*	0.672*	0.161*	0.222*	0.410*
MC_5					1	0.890*	0.259*	0.292*	0.477*
MCT						1	0.372*	0.430*	0.657*
AA							1	0.472*	0.521*
I								1	0.514*
AM									1

AA = Academic Achievement; I = Intelligence; AM = Achievement Motivation
*Correlation is significant at 0.05 level (2-tailed)

Table-43 represents the correlation matrix of Motor Creativity and its components with other three variables on the total subjects (N = 960). In all the cases the obtained 'r'-value were higher than the tabulated 'r'-value in between variable relationship; which were significant at 0.05 level. Therefore, the relationships between the variables among all the variables were statistically significant for the teenage students.

A number of investigations have been carried out by different researchers to find out the relationship between creativity and academic achievement. Most of these investigations Bagga (1973), Bedi (1974), Masih (1980), Vijaylakshmi (1980) and Jarial (1981) indicate a significantly positive relationship between the creativity of subjects and their academic achievement. Many other investigators Getzels and Jackson (1959 and 1962) observed that inspite of the difference of 23 points in mean I. Q., high creativity and high intelligence did not differ significantly in their academic achievement. Torrance (1959) in a study with students from 4 to 6 grades observed that the coefficient of correlation between academic achievement and creativity ranged from 0.37 to 0.53. Yamamoto (1964) compared the high creative group with low creative group, it was observed that the high creative group surpassed the low creative group in academic achievement. Paramesh (1973) found that there was a significantly positive relationship between creativity and subjects academic achievement. Contrary to these, there are a few studies by Holland (1961), Phatak (1962), Badrinath and Satyanarayan (1979) and Sharma (1981) where the investigators have reported that academic achievement had no significant relationship with creativity. Sandhu (1979) also found that when the effect of intelligence was controlled, academic achievement and creativity were not found to be significantly related.

The present study resembles with the study of Bagga (1973), Bedi (1974), Masih (1980), Vijaylakshmi (1980) and Jarial (1981) and differs from the studies of Holland (1961), Phatak (1962), Badrinath and Satyanayan (1979) and Sharma (1981).

A person with high convergent thinking will surely be high on intelligence, but need not always be high on creativity. Of the various studies conducted in respect of creativity and intelligence, significantly high positive relationship between creativity and intelligence has been reported in majority of the studies, Laughlim (1967), Passi (1971), Sharma (1971), Deshmukh (1980), Gakhar (1980), Passi (1971), Sharma (1971), Deshmukh (1980), Jarial (1981) found high positive relationship between creativity and intelligence. In some other studies a positive but low relationship has been reported between these two variables as by Guilford (1950), Thorndike 91963), Mackinnon (1962), and Mc-Alpine (1972). Contrary to the above mentioned studies there are a few investigations where the investigators found that the two variables were not related to each other. Das (1957, 1959), Khire (1971), Lalithamma (1973), Rawat and Agarwal (1977), Safaya (1981) observed that when the effect of academic achievement was partialled out, creativity showed no relationship to intelligence.

The present study resembles with the study of Laughlin (1967), Passi (1971), Sharma (1971), Deshmukh (1980), Gokhar and Passi (1971) but differs from the findings of Guilford (1950), Thorndike (1963), Mackinnon (1962) and Mc-Alpine (1972).

According to a study by Peek (1958) creativity is largely a result of a drive to be unique and the desire to prove superiority of the drives. Crutchfield (1961) found creative people to be highly motivated to work. Mukherjee conducted a study to measure achievement values and scientific productivity. He found that teachers having high achievement motivation values show greater scientific productivity than their colleagues whose N-ach series are low. Raina (1969) found that students who scored higher in creativity, their creativity scores were significantly higher than the low creative students.

So the present study corroborates with the studies of Crutchfield (1961), Mukherjee (1974) and Raina (1969).

Regression Equations :

Motor Creativity differs in male and female adolescent students across their age, and motor creativity has relationship with intelligence, achievement motivation and academic achievement. Hence, the regression equations are prepared according to age for both genders considering motor creativity as the dependent variable with the three independent variables, i.e., intelligence, achievement motivation and academic achievement.

Table – 44 : Multiple Correlation and Regression Equations for Girls group

Group	Regression Equations	R	R^2	s. e. e.
13- year	MC = 27.025 + 0.035 (AA) + 1.275 (INT) + 0.047 (AM)	0.894	0.799	4.05482
14-year	MC = 29.419 + 0.016 (AA) + 1.564 (INT) + 0.014 (AM)	0.875	0.765	4.66201
15-year	MC = 51.722 + 0.056 (AA) – 0.307 (INT) + 0.103 (AM)	0.549	0.301	6.02633
16-year	MC = 41.259 + 0.018 (AA) + 0.773 (INT) + 0.123 (AM)	0.836	0.698	4.06751
17-year	MC = 53.083 + 0.017 (AA) + 0.512 (INT) + 0.097 (AM)	0.456	0.208	6.29415
18-year	MC = 54.832 + 0.010 (AA) + 0.744 (INT) + 0.047 (AM)	0.452	0.204	6.08560

R= Multiple Correlation Coefficient; R^2 = Coefficient of Determination; s.e.e.=Standard error of estimate
MC = Motor Creativity; AA = Academic Achievement; INT = Intelligence; AM = Achievement Motivation

Table-44 represents the multiple correlation coefficients and regression equations for girls group to calculate the motor creativity from their academic achievement, intelligence and achievement motivation in accordance with their age. There are six regression equations, one equation for each age group teenage girl students in the table. Here, all the six multiple correlation coefficients are within the acceptable range. Therefore, motor creativity of teenage girl students can be predicted from their academic achievement, intelligence and achievement motivation.

Table – 45 : Multiple Correlation and Regression Equations for Boys group

Group	Regression Equations	R	R^2	s. e. e.
13-year	MC = 38.422 + 0.026 (AA) + 0.644 (INT) + 0.138 (AM)	0.638	0.407	5.04737
14-year	MC = 34.036 – 0.024 (AA) + 1.914 (INT) + 0.088 (AM)	0.729	0.531	6.11187
15-year	MC = 63.138 + 0.027 (AA) – 0.019 (INT) + 0.052 (AM)	0.452	0.205	6.47395
16-year	MC = 48.524 + 0.057 (AA) + 0.142 (INT) + 0.052 (AM)	0.691	0.477	5.51240
17-year	MC = 82.620 – 0.038 (AA) + 0.390 (INT) + 0.185 (AM)	0.299	0.089	5.84612
18-year	MC = 80.919 – 0.004 (AA) + 0.689 (INT) – 0.005 (AM)	0.403	0.162	5.81205

R=Multiple Correlation Coefficient; R^2 =Coefficient of Determination; s.e.e.=Standard error of estimate
MC = Motor Creativity; AA = Academic Achievement; INT = Intelligence; AM = Achievement Motivation

Table–45 comprises the multiple correlation co-efficient and regression equations for boys group to determine the motor creativity (MC) predicted from academic achievement (AA), intelligence (INT) and achievement motivation (AM). According to age group, for six age groups there are six regression equations. Here, all the six multiple correlation coefficients are within the acceptable limit. Therefore, motor creativity of teenage boy students can be predicted from their academic achievement, intelligence and achievement motivation.

CHAPTER – V
SUMMARY, CONCLUSION AND RECOMMENDATION

5.1 Summary

Creativity is a general constellation of supporting intellectual and personality traits and problem solving traits that help expression of creative behaviour in individual. Genetic factors notwithstanding, the environmental factors can not be ignored. Creativity is universal; it exerts influence on any field of human endeavour.

Creative thinking starts with a problematic situation. The field of motor creativity offers numerous problematic situations. The universality of creativity is manifested in the motor activity arena too; and it provides rich resources for stimulating motor creativity. Creativity in motor activity i.e. motor creativity is one expression of the universality of human creativity.

Individual differences do exist. It is a well established fact and well known theory. This theory is also manifested in motor creativity. Motor Creativity differs from individual to individual; and differs at various ages. Creativity, although universal, is probably influenced by age, gender and area.

Movement and exercise are very basic to human living. They affect the development of human personality in various ways, and in the process expose creative motor responses.

Various factors may affect creativity, and for that matter, motor creativity. Some such factors like age, gender, area and intelligence, achievement motivation and academic achievement may affect creativity and motor creativity.

Intelligence is the aggregate or global capacity of the individual to act purposefully, to think rationally and to deal effectively with his environment.

Due to varying influence of age on gender and area there may probably be varying degrees of creative motor responses among individuals of different age groups.

Freedom of participation is also one factor for gathering experience and expressing creative imagination, often through motor movements. The girls gather less experience than the boys as the boys get more freedom than the girls in our society. Do they differ in motor creativity?

With such a perspective the researcher felt stimulated to undertake this study.

The purpose of the present study was to assess creative motor responses, intellectual ability, achievement motivation and academic achievement ability of the subjects; to find out the relationship between the selected parameters in respect of age, gender, area and to focus motor creativity in relation to them; to predict which one of the selected variables was closely related to motor creativity; to assess the difference of intelligence between the hill and plane subjects; to predict influence of age upon motor creativity components and on total motor creativity, if any; to assess gender influence or area influence if any on the early adolescent (13 to 15 years) and late adolescent (16 to 19 years) groups on the determinant variables.

The study might throw new light on creative motor responses in relation to intelligence, achievement motivation, academic achievement, age, gender and locality. Although the study was delimited to a selected age range between thirteen to eighteen years with a sample selected from a rather narrow population (960), 480 males and 480 females from two geo-physically distinctly different districts of West Bengal.

The scope of creativity needs more careful and critical study so that educational experiences can be designed to stimulate the expression of creativeness in a variety of appropriate ways. The researcher reviewed quite a good number of research works of Indian and researchers of abroad from books, journals and internet. Most of the research works were related to creativity and motor creativity related research work were very few in number. Creativity was studied from different angles, i.e. Creativity and age, Creativity and gender, Creativity and area. Relationship between creativity and other influencing factors like intelligence, achievement motivation and academic achievement also observed for in-depth knowledge and understanding on creativity and its various aspects.

To accomplish the purpose of the study questionnaires for intelligence and achievement motivation were adopted. The academic achievement of the students was collected from the school marks register and a test battery of motor creativity consisting of five test items was taken. Nine hundred and sixty students 13 years to 19 years (13^+–18^+ years) of age of both boys and girls of hill and plane area were selected as the subjects. For each age group 40 boys and 40 girls, both from plane area and hill area, were randomly selected.

For collection of data the criterion measures considered were - motor creativity, intelligence, academic achievement and achievement motivation. Academic achievement was recorded from the marks register of the schools. Motor creativity was measured by Wyrick Test of Motor Creativity (1966) redesigned and standardized by Ghosh and Bhattacharya (1988).

The researcher used a standardized questionnaire for measuring intelligence test framed by Bhattacharya (1991) and achievement motivation by questionnaire for

Achievement Motivation Test (n-Ach) Deo-Mohan's (2002).

The written test for intelligence and achievement motivation were conducted in groups of forty eight, and the motor creativity tests were conducted individually in separate rooms so that no subjects could see the performance of other subjects. The practical tests were taken on different days. After administering the tests, item-wise scoring was done separately. Each valid response had one work. The summation of scores obtained in all the five test items gave the total score of motor creativity.

By following the all-or-none principle the responses in intelligence and achievement motivation questionnaire were converted into numerical scores.

Data thus collected were statistically analysed and interpreted for finding the results of the study. At first the mean and SD were computed, then analysis of variance was computed to determine influence of the variables (age, gender, area) in motor creativity of teen age students. The pair-wise comparison was computed by LSD test. The correlations between motor creativity and intelligence, achievement motivation and academic achievement for the same age groups (13 to 18 years) and for early and late adolescent groups were found out to observe the relationship among the variables.

The mean and SD of the scores of motor creativity components and motor creativity total for 13-year age group of total plane and hill areas were 19.13 ± 2.22, 15.47 ± 1.99, 13.62 ± 1.98, 12.06 ± 1.99, 21.75 ± 2.86 and 81.90 ± 7.75 for MC_1, MC_2, MC_3, MC_4, MC_5 and Motor Creativity total respectively. For 14-year age group the mean and SD were 19.18 ± 2.14, 15.69 ± 2.16, 13.77 ± 1.98, 12.52 ± 2.04, 22.78 ± 3.50, 83.91 ± 9.08 for MC_2, MC_3, MC_4, MC_5 and Motor Creativity total respectively. For 15-year age group it were 19.50 ± 1.85, 15.91 ± 2.05, 14.38 ± 1.95, 13.73 ± 1.75, 25.28 ± 3.43 and 88.82 ± 7.15 for MC_1, MC_2, MC_3, MC_4, MC_5 and Motor Creativity total respectively. For 16-year age group the mean and SD were 18.90 ± 2.18, 15.45 ± 1.89, 13.96 ± 1.81, 13.40 ± 1.83, 27.05 ± 5.32 and 88.85 ± 8.67 respectively. For 17-year age group the scores were 20.02 ± 2.20, 16.95 ± 1.77, 14.71 ± 1.61, 13.90 ± 1.87, 23.92 ± 3.26 and 89.64 ± 6.61 respectively.

For 18 year age group the scores were 20.31 ± 2.05, 17.78 ± 2.41, 16.21 ± 2.20, 15.74 ± 2.59, 23.81 ± 2.68 and 93.68 ± 8.96 respectively. The mean and SD of boys and girls of hill area and boys and girls of plane area were 19.39 ± 2.30, 15.92 ± 2.31. The mean and SD scores for all the five motor creativity components and motor creativity total of the boys and girls of hill area were 19.39 ± 2.30, 15.92 ± 2.31, 14.27 ± 2.38, 13.66 ± 2.84, 24.38 ± 4.17, 87.67 ± 9.73 and for plane area it was 19.62 ± 2.02, 16.50 ± 2.10, 14.62 ± 1.80, 13.45 ± 1.70, 23.79 ± 3.79 and 87.96 ± 8.12 respectively.

Age was found to be the most effective variable in motor creativity. Motor creativity increased with age during adolescent stage.

When gender was considered the boys group was found superior to the girls group in motor creativity.

When age and area were considered the students achieved high scores in motor creativity with the increase of age and the plane area students were superior to the hill area students.

Except in MC_1, the early adolescent and the late adolescent students did differ in all the motor creativity components.

Motor creativity of the early adolescent and the late adolescents were positively related with intelligence, achievement motivation and academic achievement. Five components of motor creativity were positively correlated among themselves in teenage students.

The correlation between academic achievement and achievement motivation of the total group is 0.472, achievement motivation and intelligence is 0.514. The correlations were found significant at 0.05 level. The correlation matrix of the boys and girls between academic achievement and intelligence is 0.492, intelligence and achievement motivation is 0.561 and 0.379, motor creativity and intelligence is 0.580 and 0.515, motor creativity and achievement motivation is 0.382 and 0.487, and motor creativity and academic achievement is 0.229 and 0.550. The regression was conducted to predict the level of Motor Creativity from the influencing variables like intelligence, achievement motivation and academic achievement.

The exception that was found in 16 years that is a drip in motor creativity which might have been due to two reasons :

1) The subjects of the 16 year age group were class X students. As the students had their test examinations prior to· school Final Examination within a few days after the dates of investigation, their mental set up was engrossed with their studies. The unusual result of this age group might have been due to a sort of casual approach on the part of the subjects.

2) The number of the subjects involved in the age group 16+ was not a big one to represent the population of the same age group.

Major Findings on Motor Creativity according to Age

When age was considered as the source of variation in MC we can see a gradual increase in motor creativity scores during adolescence. However at the age of 16 a drip in motor creativity was observed.

When gender was considered we see that the girls differed from the boys in motor creativity. The boys group were superior than the girls group.

When area was considered, motor creativity as a whole did not differ between plane and hill area students. However in three MC components differences were observed.

When age is considered a significant difference is found in MC_1 (originality), in gender the calculated F-value showed significant difference. Hence a significant difference was found between boys and girls in MC_1 (originality). There was no influence of area on originality MC_1 (originality) among teenage students.

Significant difference in MC_2 (flexibility) was found among the six age groups of the study. In MC_2 (flexibility) a significant difference between boys and girls are found. There is an influence of area on MC_2 (flexibility) among the teenage students. When age and area both were considered a significant difference was observed.

Age reveals a significant difference in MC_3 (ISP) among the six age groups. Boys and girls showed significant difference in MC_3 (ISP). Area had an influence among the teenage students. When age and gender, gender and area were considered significant differences were observed. But when age, gender and area were considered combinedly no significant difference was observed among the six age groups.

Significant difference was observed in MC_4 (fluency) when age was considered. Gender and area showed no significant difference in MC_4 (fluency). When age and gender, age and area, gender and area considered significant differences were observed. When age, gender and area were considered significant differences were found.

Age, gender and area had a significant difference in MC_5 (elaboration). When age and gender, gender and area, age and area; age, gender and area were taken into consideration significant differences were observed.

Age and gender showed significant difference in MC total, whereas area had no significant difference. When age and gender, gender and area, age and area; age, gender and area were considered significant differences were observed.

The relationship between motor creativity total (MCT) and the other three variables i.e. academic achievement (AA), Achievement motivation (AM) and intelligence (I) among the total boys (N = 480) and girls (N = 480) group is represented in Table 39. In boys group the relationship between motor creativity variables were found to be significant in all the cases except the two relationships those were between MC_5 (elaboration) to MC_2 (flexibility) and MC_5 (elaboration) to MC_3 (ISP). The relationship with other variables of Intelligence and Motivation were found significant. In case of girls group the relationship between motor creativity and its components with other variables were found significant except between MC_2 (flexibility) to MC_5 (elaboration).

When total subjects (N = 960) were considered for multiple correlation analysis on motor creativity and its components with other three variables, it was observed that the relationship between the variables and among all the variables were statistically significant for the teenage students.

Major Findings on Motor Creativity in Early and Late Adolescence

In all the motor creativity components and in motor creativity total late adolescent boys and late adolescent girls were better than the early adolescent boys and early adolescent girls. Significant difference were observed among the two groups (early and late teenage) in MC_1 (originality) and also in gender. But area showed no significant difference among the age groups. When interaction between group and gender, gender and area were considered significant difference were observed in MC_1 whereas no significant difference was observed in the interaction between gender and area; group, gender and area were considered.

In MC_2 (flexibility) significant differences were observed in between groups (early and late adolescence), gender and area. When interaction between group and gender, gender and area were considered significant differences were observed but no significant differences were observed when the interaction between group and area as well as group, gender and area were considered.

In MC_3 (ingenious solution to problems) group, gender and area when taken individually showed significant difference. The interaction between group and gender, group and area, gender and area also showed significant difference only when group, gender and area were combinedly considered no significant differences were observed.

Significant differences were observed in MC_4 (fluency) when group was considered but when area and gender were considered no significant difference was observed. In interaction between group and gender; group and area, gender and area significant differences were observed but in interaction between group, gender and area no significant differences were observed.

In MC_5 (elaboration) group, gender and area as well as in all the interactions i.e., between group and gender, group and area, gender and area; and in group, gender and area significant differences were observed.

In MCT group and gender showed significant differences but area showed no significant difference. In interaction between group and gender, group and area, gender and area significant differences were observed whereas in interaction between group, gender and area no difference was observed.

The relationship between motor creativity total (MCT) and the other three variables, i.e. academic achievement (AA), Intelligence (I) and achievement motivation (AM) of early adolescent boys and girls were significantly correlated.

In late adolescent boys group the relationship between Motor Creativity and its components were found to be significant in all the cases except the relationships between MC_1 and MC_5 which was statistically not significant.

The relationship between academic achievement and the remaining variables were found to be significant in two cases that were for MC_4 and MC_5 and MCT along with the remaining motor creativity components i.e., MC_1, MC_2 and MC_3 the relationships were not significant.

5.2 Conclusion

After an analytical estimate of the results the conclusions of this study are drawn in two ways :
i) Difference in motor creativity with respect to age, gender, area and their interactions.
ii) Relationship between motor creativity and other variables among the teenage students as whole, teenage male and female students and among early and late adolescent male and female students.

1. On difference in Motor Creativity :

i) Motor creativity increased according to age during adolescence. However at the age of sixteen a drip in motor creativity was observed. Late adolescent students were superior in motor creativity than early adolescent students when they were classified according to early and late adolescent groups.
ii) Boys and girls differed in motor creativity. The boys group was superior than the girls group.

iii) Motor creativity as a whole did not differ between plane and hill area students. However among the five motor creativity components the differences were observed in three components.
iv) Motor creativity did differ according to age and gender. The boys group at the whole adolescent stage from 13 to 19 years were superior in motor creativity than the girls of the same age group.
v) Motor creativity also did differ according to gender and area. The plane boys were superior than the hill boys and from the girls of both plane and hill areas.
vi) When age and area were considered the students did differ. The higher was the age group of the students the higher was motor creativity and also the plane area students were superior than the hill area students. When the students were classified in early and late adolescent groups they did differ in all the motor creativity components except in originality (MC_1).
vii) When motor creativity was understood in terms of age, gender and area, except in one component originality (MC_1) the student did differ. On the other hand in early and late adolescent group except in elaboration (MC_5), no difference in motor creativity aspects were observed.

2. On Relationship between Motor Creativity and other Variables :

i) Motor creativity of teenage students was positively related to intelligence, achievement motivation and academic achievement.
ii) In adolescent boys motor creativity also was positively related with intelligence, academic achievement and achievement motivation.
iii) In adolescent boys motor creativity also was positively related with intelligence, academic achievement and achievement motivation.
iv) Motor creativity of early adolescent boys and girls was positively related to intelligence, achievement motivation and academic achievement.
v) In late adolescent boys and girls motor creativity was positively related with intelligence, achievement motivation and academic achievement.
vi) In most of the cases the five components of motor creativity were positively correlated among themselves in teenage students.

5.3 Recommendations

Considering the various aspects of the present study, the following recommendations may be made :

i) The subjects of this study is confined among the teenagers i.e. 13 to 18 years age group only, it would be interesting to note the findings of future research work done among the 7 to 9 years age group, 10 to 12 years age group and also among the college students.

ii) This work may be done among the players of different games to find out if motor creativity levels have any influence upon performance of the particular game players.

iii) For objective measurement of motor creativity tests, the video recorder may prove useful, particularly for measuring originality and flexibility.

iv) The subjects of this study are normal school going children; it may also be explored with the physically challenged students.

v) A nomogram may be constructed for assessing motor creativity on the basis of intelligence, achievement motivation and academic achievement scores.

vi) A standard test battery of motor creativity with scoring key, applicable for different age groups may be constructed.

vii) The researcher in this study tried to find out if there is any relationship between motor creativity and intelligence, achievement motivation, academic achievement. Other influencing factors of motor creativity like personality, socio-economic states, and birth order may be considered for correlation studies.

viii) This work is confined among the hill and the plane teenage students it would be interesting to note the findings of future research work done among the rural and urban teenage students.

ix) Physical educator and coaches may consider inclusion of motor creativity as a criterion for selection of players, particularly because motor creativity seem to be an important component in that type of games where the movements are not pre-determined.

BIBLIOGRAPHY

Books

Arnold, J. E. (1962-b): Useful Creative Techniques: A Source Book of Creative Thinking. New York: Charles Scribners Sons.

Buch, M. B. (1987). Third Survey of Research in Education. New Delhi: National Council of Educational Research and Training.

Bucher, C. A. (1979). Foundations of Physical Education (8th Ed.). New York: The C. V. Mosby Company.

Cattell, R. B. (1947). Personality and Motivation, Structures and Measurement. New York: World Book.

Cratty, Bryant J. (1973). Movement Behaviour and Motor Learning. Philadelphia: Lea and Febiger.

Crow, L. D. & Crow, A. (1973). Educational Psychology. Delhi: Eurasia Publishing House Pvt. Ltd..

Das, N. G. (1986) Statistical Methods. Calcutta: Das and Co.

Datta, N. K. & Lal, G. (1977). The Creativity Potential and Education. Ambala Cantt.: Indian Book Agency.

Davis, E. C. & G. (1961). A. Logan. Biophysical Values of Muscular Activity. Dubuque, Iowa : William C. Brown Company Publishers.

Deo, P. & Mohan, A. (2002). Manual for Deo-Mohan Achievement Motivation Scale. Agra: National Psychological Corporation.

Edwards, A. L. (1971). Experimental Design in Psychological Research (3rd Ed.). Amerind Publishing Co. Pvt. Ltd., pp. 422 - 425.

Fleishman, E. A. (1964). The Structure and Measurement of physical fitness. Englewood Cliffs.

Freeman, F. S. (1950). Theory and Practice of Psychological Testing (3rd Ed.). New York, Holt. pp. 518.

Garrett, H. E. (1979). Statistics in Psychology and Education (Tenth Indian Reprint). Bombay: Vakils, Feffer and Simons.

Getzels, J. W. (1962). Creativity and Intelligence, Exploration with gifted students. New York: John Wiley.

Goodenough, F. L. (1949). Mental Testing. New York: Rinehart and Company Inc.

Guilford, J. P. (1968). Intelligence, Creativity and their educational implications. San Diego, California: Robert R. Knapp.

Gupta, S. C. (1985). Psychology Applied to General Education and Physical Education. Meerut : Pragati Prakashan

Harrison, Clarke, H. (1976). Application of Measurement to Health and Physical Education. (5th Ed.). New Jersey: Prentice Hall, Inc.

Havighurst, R. J. (1953). Human Development and Education. London: Longmans Green and Co. Ltd..

Johnson, B. L. & Nelson, J. K. (1982). Practical Measurements for Evaluation in Physical Education (3rd Ed.). Delhi: Surjeet Publishing .

Kamalesh, M. L. & Sangral, M. S. (1988). Principles and History of Physical Education. Ludhiana: Prakash Brothers.

Klafs, C. E. & Arnhelm, D. D. (1977). Modern Principles of Athletic Training (Fourth Edition). Saint Louis: The C. V. Mosby Company.

Larson, L. A. (1971). Encyclopaedia of Sports Sciences and Medicine. New York: The Macmillan Company.

Layman, E. M. (1960). Contribution to Exercise and Sports to Mental Health and Social Adjustment. New York: Harper and Brothers.

Lehman, H. (1953): Age and Achievements. Princeton University Press.

Lytton, Hugh. Creativity and Education (1971). London: Rutledge and Kegen Paul.

Mangal, S. K. (1987). Educational Psychology. Jalandhar City: Prakash Brother.

Mangal, S. K. (1987). Statistics in Psychology and Education, New Delhi: Tata McGraw-Hill Publishing Company Limited.

Passy, B. K. (1982). Creativity in Education. Agra: National Psychological Corporation.

Roy, S. (1984). A Text book on Educational Psychology. Calcutta: Soma Book Agency.

Sansanwal, D. N. & Jarial, G. S. (1986). Creativity and Age. Creativity Newsletter.

Singh (1978). A. Is Intelligence inherited? New Delhi: National Council of Educational Research and Training.

Skinner, Charles E. (Ed.). Educational Psychology.

Stern, W. (1914). Psychological Methods of Testing Intelligence. Baltimore: Warwick and York, Inc.

Terman, L. M. & Merrill, M. M. (1937). Measuring Intelligence. Boston: Houghton Miffin Company.

Varducci, R. M. (1980). Measurement Concept in Physical Education. St. Louis: C. V. Mosby Co.

Vernon, P. E (1970). Creativity Selected Readings. Middlesex, Emotion (2), 226 – 232 (Gr. Britain): The Chaucer Press Ltd.

Journals / Periodicals / Dissertations

Achmidt, R A. (1971). Retroactive interference and amount of original learning in verbal and motor task. *Research Quarterly*, 42 (3): 314.

Adoock, C. J. & Martin, W. A. (1971). Flexibility and creativity. *Journal of General Psychology*, 85(1): 71 – 76.

Akinboye, I. O. (1982). Correlates of testing time, age and sex in the Nigerians: Performance on the Torrance Test of Creativity. *Journal of Psychological Research,* 26 (I) : 1 – 5.

Awasthy, H. (1979). A study of creativity, intelligence, scholastic achievement and other factors of socio-economic status. *M. Ed. Dissertation*, Indore University.

Badrinath, S. & Satyanarayan, S. B. (1979). Correlates of creative thinking of high school students. *Creative News Letter*, 778 (1&2) : 22 – 27.

Barret, H. E. & Koch, H. L. (1930). Pedagogical Seminar. *Journal of Genetic Psychology*, 37.

Beverage, S. K. (1973). The relationship among motor creativity, movement satisfaction and the utlilization of certain movement factor of second grade children. Ph. D. Thesis. The Ohio State University. *Dissertation Abstract International*, 35 (7): 7022A, 1975.

Binet, A. & Simon, T. (1980). Le development de I. intelligence Chzles infants, Le' Annec *Psychologique*, XIV.

Bockrath, D. A. (1980). The relationship between reaction time and both intelligence and achievement in Normal, Gifted, EMR and LD populations. Ph. D. Thesis. Kent State University, pp. 157. *Dissertation Abstract International*, 45(2): 3589A, 1985.

Brennan, M. A. (1977). An investigation into the relationship between creative ability in dance, field independence – Dependence and Creativity. Ph. D. Thesis. The University of Wisconsin. *Dissertation Abstract International*, 37(7): 4209A ,1976.

Bruininks, Roberts H. & Feldman David, H. (1970): Creativity, intelligence and achievement among disadvantaged children. Psychology in the Schools, 7(3): 260 – 264.

Buch, M. B. (1987). Third Survey of Research in Education (1978–83). New Delhi: NCERT.

Carlier, Michale (1971). Flexibility a dimensional analysis of a modality of divergent thinking. Perceptual and Motor Skills, 32(2): 447 – 48.

Clemente Franco Justo (Spain). (2008). Creative relaxation, motor creativity, self-concept in a sample of children from early childhood education. *Electronic Journal of Research in Educational Psychology,* 14 (1) 5 – 16.

Darden, E. & Shapple, R. T. (1972). Performance by Males and females on three motor tasks under standard and mirror reversal condition. *Research Quarterly,* 43: 460.

Dharmangadan, B. (1981).Creativity in relation to sex, age and local. *Psychology Studies,* 26 (1): 28 – 33.

Dickson, T. L. (1973). A study of the effects of a programme of group creativity in Physical Education. M. S. in Physical Education Thesis, Spring Field College, U. S. A. *Compiled Research in Health, Physical Education and Recreation,* 15: 128, 1972.

Evans, E. E. (1983). Attitude of gifted midday schools students toward Physical Education in Connecticut Public School. Ph. D. Thesis, The University of Connecticut, *Dissertation Abstract International,* 44(2): 427A, 1983.

Freeman, Frank S. (1950). Theory and practice of psychological testing. New York : Holt, pp. 518.

Fleming, A. W. The Relationships of Creativity Attitude towards Physical Education and Physical Education Activity skill of Physical Education students and their Teachers. Ph. D. Thesis, University of Wisconsin, USA.

Gakher, S. (1974). Creativity in Relation to Age and Sex. *Journal of Education and Psychology,* 32:122.

Ghosh, M. C. (1988). A study in creativity, motor ability and motor creativity of adolescent students. Ph. D. Thesis. University of Kalyani.

Glover, E. G. A motor creativity test for college women. Ed. Thesis. University of North Caroline at Greensboro, p. 2033.

Gokhan, N. (1977). Coefficient of correlation between physical ability and mental development. *Journal of Sports Medicine and Physical Fitness. Torino* : Minerva Medica, Vol. 17 (2).

Gupta, A. K. (1977). A study of the relationship of creativity with self-concept among the school going children of 12 plus in Jammu city. *Ph. D. Thesis,* Punjab University.

Harney, D. M. & Parkar, R. (1972). Effects of social reinforcement, subject sex and experimenter sex on children motor performance. *Research Quarterly,* 43(2): 187, 1972.

Hocevar, D. (1980). Intelligence divergent thinking and creativity. Intelligence, 4: 25 – 40.

Horn, J. L. & Cattle, R. B. (1966a). Refinement and Test of the Theory of Fluid and Crystallised Intelligence : 57, 253 – 270.

Hussin, M. G. (1974). Creativity and Sex Difference. *Psychological Statistics*, 9(2):127–129.

Hwang, Ren-Lai. (1987). The creative effectiveness of movement and music in fifth grade art class motivations. Ph. D. Thesis, University of Georgia. *Dissertation Abstract International*, 47(9): 2957–58, 1986.

Irvin, Melva E. (1977). A comparison of the performance of primary grade students on self-concept, locus of control and motor creativity in two different physical education programs. Ph. D. Thesis. University of Utah. 1976. *Dissertation Abstract International*, 37(7): 42313A, 1977.

Jarial, G. S. & Sharma, A. K. (1981). Sex Roles in Verbal Creativity Thinking Abilities. *Psycho-Lingua,* 2(1): 15 – 18.

Joshi, R. J. (1974). A study of creativity and some personality traits of the intellectually gifted high school students. Ph. D. Thesis, MSU.

Justo, C. F. (2007). Creative relaxation, motor creativity, self concept in a sample of children from early childhood education, 152 (2): 402 – 404.

Laston, D. J. (1971). A comparison of motor creativity with verbal creativity and figural creativity of black culturally deprived children. Ph. D. Thesis, University of North Caroline. *Dissertation Abstract International*, 32(5) 2458-A.

Le-Breck, C. K. (1991). Development of motor creativity test for elementary school children (K-3). Ph. D. Thesis, University of Minnesota. *Dissertation Abstract International,* 47(8).

Lubin, E. N. (1979). Motor creativity test of pre-school deaf children. Ph. D. Thesis. Texas Women University. *Dissertation Abstract International*, 40(I):154.

Lynn Richard (2004). Testing the development theory of sex difference in intelligence on 12 – 18 years old, Elsevier, 36(1): 75 – 82.

Lynn, R., Allik, J., Pullman, H. & Laidra, K. (2004). Sex differences on the progressive matrices among adolescents: some data from Estonia. Personality and Individual Differences, 36, 1249-1257.

Marta Casterier & Carlota Torrents. Identifying and Analyzing Motor Skill Responses in Body Movement and Dance. *Creativity Research Journal*, 30th Issue.

McCutchen, M. G. (1979). Expert determination of knowledge and skills essential to the elementary classroom teacher for the instruction of creative dance. *Dissertation Abstract International*,39 (12): 7224-A.

Mehrotra (1986). A Study of Relationship between intelligence, socio-economic status, anxiety, personality achievement of high school students. Ph. D. Education. Kan University. In M. B. Buch's Fourth Survey of Research in Education, Article 952.

Nobel, M. L. (1973). For the love of movement through creative dance in Physical Education. M. S. in Physical Education Thesis. Spring-field College, USA. *Compiled Research in Health Physical Education and Recreation,* 15:130, 1972

O'Neill, D. K. V. S. (1982). The development of a refined movement analysis and its relationship to motor creativity among grade two children. Ed. D. Thesis. University of Oregon. *Dissertation Abstract International*, 43(2): 396A, 1982.

Oxadine, J. B. (1969). Effect of mental and physical practice on the learning of three motor skills. *Research Quarterly*, 40(4): 755 – 763.

Pagona, B., Anastasia Makri, A. & Mylonas, K. (2009). Creative Children often have Difficulty in Forming Self Concept. *Creativity Research Journal,* 2: 104 – 110.

Pearlman, C. (1983). A theoretical model for creativity. *Journal of Education,* 108(3): 294 – 305.

Philip, J. A. (1969). Comparison of motor creativity with figural and verbal creativity and selected motor skills. *Research Quarterly*, 40(1): 163 – 173.

Raina, M. K. (1970). A study of creativity in teachers. *Psychological Studies*, 15(1&2) : 28 – 33.

Raina, M. K. (1971). Verbal and nonverbal creative thinking ability – A study in sex differences. *Journal of Education and Psychology*, 29(3):175 – 179.

Rajput, A. S. (1984). Study of Academic Achievement of Students in Mathematics in relation of their Intelligence, Motivation and Socio-economic Status. Ph. D. Thesis Education. Pan University, In M. B. Fourth Survey of Research in Education. Article 967.

Ramire, E. H. (1980). Creative movement – An analysis of methods used by experts. Ed. D. Thesis, Brighem Young University. *Dissertation Abstract International*, 41(6): 2500-A, 1980.

Robberts, M. (1971). The inter-relationship of the creative process and creative personality to activities and methodology in Physical Education. Ph. D. Thesis, University of North Caroline at Greensboro. *Dissertation Abstract International*, 32(4): 1094-A , 1971.

Rogers, M. S. (1985). Creativity and play materials: The origins and development of creativity in preschool children. Ph. D. Thesis, Texas A & M University. *Dissertation Abstract International*, 45(12): 3589A , 1984.

Rose, A. J. L. C. (1983). Effect of creative dance movement of a specific cognitive skill. *Dissertation Abstract International*, 44(3) 669-A.

Rowe, P. J. (1977). Motor creativity mildly mentally retarded preschool children. Ph. D. Thesis, Texas Women's University. *Dissertation Abstract International,* 37(7):4216A,

Sansanwal, D. N. & Jarial, G. S. (1980). Creativity and Age. *Creativity News Letter.*

Schmidt, R. A. (1963). Consistency of response components as a function of selected motor variables. *Research Quarterly*, 40(3): 561 – 66.

Sharma, A. K. (1979). A study of creativity in relation to intelligence, personality, socio economic status and sex of high school students of Indore city. *M. Ed. Dissertation.* Indore University.

Sharma, J. (1965) Creativity and its Relationship with an Intrinsic Value Inventory. *Selected Readings*, Suffolk: The Chaucer Press Ltd.

Singh, A. (1978). Its Intelligence Inherited? New Delhi, NCERT, p. 4.

Trevles. E., Matsouka, O., Zachopoulou E. (2003). Early Child Development and Care,173(5):535 – 543.

Trigy, M. G. (1979). The effect of varying amounts of creative modern dance activities on creative thinking ability and self-concept. *Dissertation Abstract International*, 39(2): 722.

Truhon, S. A. (1983). Playfulness, play and creativity – A path analytic model. *Journal of Genetic Psychology*, 143(1):19 – 28.

Twillie, G. B. (1981). The Effective of Creative Dance on the School Readiness of Five Year Old Children. Ph. D. Thesis. Texas Women University. *Dissertation Abstract International*, 41(2): 5025-A , 1980

Vernon, P. E (1970). Creativity: Selected Readings, Middlesex, Emotion. 5(2), 226-232.

Wang, J. Hui-Tzu. (1998). The effects of a creative movement program on motor creativity of children, ages three to five. *Dissertation Abstract International*, 35(3): 274.

White, W. (1971). Relationship of aspect of body concept, creativity and sports proficiency. ph. d. thesis, university of Wisconsin. *Dissertation Abstract International*, 32(2):777-A, 1971.

Wilson, T. R. (1985). The effect of creative movement and contact improvisation experience on self-awareness. Ph. D. Thesis, University of Houston. *Dissertation Abstract International*, 46(6):1556-A,1985.

Other Online Resources :

Georgios, L., Evgunia, T., Thoedora T., S. D. P. (2003). "Development of Motor Theory, Flexibility and Originality Through Motor Creativity in Kindergarten" http://www.hape.gr /emag/vol1_3/hape37.pdf

May, Rollo (1974). http://www.andyeklund.com/creativestreak/2010/02/definitions-of-creativity.html

Kellor, James (1971). http://www.andyeklund.com/creativestreak/2010/02/definitions-of-creativity.html

Uguroglu (1982). http://en.scientificcommons.org/3057152

Grigoryadis, Alexandra (1989). http://www.researchgate.net/publication /35332486 _Motivation_ and_achievement_of_Greek_students_in_English_as_a_foreign_ language_as_seen_from_the_perspective_of_gender_and_parental_education_

Wiener (1986). http://www.instructionaldesign.org/theories/attribution-theory.html.

Pelachano (1972), libwiki.ru / index.php?n=Main.Personalityand Intellectual Competence191

Khatena (1987), books.google.co.in/books?isbn=0898628938

Rajput, A. S. (1984), books.google.co.in/books?isbn=8183563341

Oudeyer P-Y, Kaplan , F. & Hafner, V. (2007) Intrinsic Motivation Systems for Autonomous Mental Development, IEEE Transactions on Evolutionary Computation, 11(2), pp. 265—286. http://www.pyoudeyer.com/ims.pdf

Charles E. Skinner (1951), Educational Psychology (ed.), Prentice-Hall, Winsted, Conn, http://www.biblio.com/books/214946194.html

APPENDIX – I
TEST OF MOTOR CREATIVITY

1. How many different types of movements of the upper part of the body can you make, while keeping the lower part of the body fixed, within a time of 3 minutes?

2.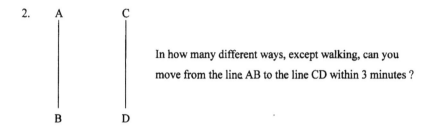

   In how many different ways, except walking, can you move from the line AB to the line CD within 3 minutes?

3. While keeping balance on a narrow base, how many movements can you perform within 3 minutes?

4. In how many different ways can you hit the target 'T' from the line AB, with a ball, by using any part of the body? Time to be allowed: 3 minutes

5. Station

A	C	a. From standing position
		b. From sitting position
		c. From supine position
B	D	d. From prone position

How many exercises can you perform in all the stations, maintaining the particular body position at the respective stations, within 5 minutes? You may perform any number of exercise, at any particular station and devote your own time at any station. But after every one minute you will be orally indicated about time.

CPSIA information can be obtained
at www.ICGtesting.com
Printed in the USA
BVHW051951301222
655313BV00014B/1577